Hemisphere Publishing Corporation
1025 Vermont Ave., N.W., Washington, D.C. 20005

Distributed solely by Halsted Press, a Division of John Wiley & Sons, Inc., New York.

1 2 3 4 5 6 7 8 9 0   D O D O   7 8 4 3 2 1 0 9 8 7 6

Library of Congress Cataloging in Publication Data

Bar-Tal, Daniel
    Prosocial behavior.

    Bibliography: p.
    Includes indexes.
    1. Helping behavior. 2. Altruism. I. Title.
[DNLM: 1. Social behavior. HM276 B283p]
BF637.H4B37   155.2'32   75-43624
ISBN 0-470-15223-0

Printed in the United States of America

PROSOCIAL BEHAVIOR

theory and research

Daniel Bar-Tal
Tel-Aviv University

 **HEMISPHERE PUBLISHING
CORPORATION**

Washington   London

A HALSTED PRESS BOOK

JOHN WILEY & SONS

New York   London   Sydney   Toronto

TO MY WIFE YAFFA AND THE TWINS, WHO
"AGREED" TO BE BORN AFTER THE WRITING
OF THE BOOK WAS FINISHED.

CONTENTS

PREFACE

Altruistic behavior has always fascinated me. Although for many years this interest relied only on common sense, the question of why some individuals are altruistic and others are not often absorbed my thinking. Martin Greenberg, my first advisor during graduate study at the University of Pittsburgh, introduced me to the systematic study of prosocial behavior. Our lengthy discussions stimulated my efforts to understand this phenomenon; out of these efforts this book was written.

Irene Frieze, Joe Golin, Gary Koeske, and John Levine of the Department of Psychology at the University of Pittsburgh encouraged me to extend and to publish this work, which was initially written as a comprehensive exam. Len Saxe, my friend and colleague, offered much encouragement during the trying period of writing and revising.

I am indebted to Alan Gross, who agreed to comment on the whole manuscript, and to Kenneth Gergen, who made important suggestions after reading a summary of the manuscript. Although I owe much to these individuals, the shortcomings of the book are entirely mine.

In addition, I am grateful to Louise Stobicki, who did all the reference work for the book, and to Terri Komar and Terry Smith, two secretaries of the Learning Research and Development Center, University of Pittsburgh, who typed drafts of the manuscript. I must also acknowledge the great help of Evelyn Pettit, of Hemisphere Publishing Corporation, and of William E. Pettit in editing the book. The Learning Research and Development Center of the University of Pittsburgh very generously provided me with material support and secretarial services during the period when this book was written.

Finally, I owe many thanks to my wife, Yaffa, who let me work until late at night while she took over all the responsibilities involved in our return to Israel.

Daniel Bar-Tal

1

WHAT IS PROSOCIAL BEHAVIOR?

Story One

John drove into the parking area of a large supermarket near his home, parked the car, and walked toward the entrance of the supermarket. As he approached the door, he noticed a Salvation Army kettle in front of the entrance; standing beside it was a woman wearing a Salvation Army cape and hat. She did not make any verbal plea, just stood and looked at the passing shoppers. Most of the people passed as if they did not notice her or the kettle, hurrying into the store or hurrying out to load their cars with groceries. Some glanced at the woman but didn't stop. Only one person put some coins in the kettle before entering the store. John felt sorry for the woman and decided to contribute several dimes. He put his hand into his pocket but it was empty. Standing beside the kettle, he decided he could not disappoint her. He put his hand into his other pocket, pulled out his wallet, took out a dollar, and put it in the kettle.

Story Two

Mary traveled to work by subway. One hot summer day the subway car was filled as usual with people going downtown. All the seats were occupied and Mary, with several dozen others, was standing in the passage. The heat, the humidity, and lack of fresh air made this trip especially unpleasant. Mary noticed an old man across from her swaying from side to side with his eyes closed. He appeared to be about 70 years old and he was obviously having difficulty standing in the crowded car. His face was sweating and very pale. Mary thought he was close to collapsing and decided to ask someone to give him a seat. But before she could open her mouth, the old man fell to the floor. Without hesitation, Mary knelt beside him. Shouting to the other people to make room, she opened his shirt. The train rolled into one of the stations and Mary asked a man standing beside her to help lift the old man and take him off the train. Mary grasped the old man's shoulders and, pushing other passengers aside, she and the other man made their way to the station platform. They put the old man on an empty bench and Mary, seeing that he was still unconscious, ran for water. On her way she asked the station clerk to call for an ambulance and to direct her to the water cooler. She wet her handkerchief and ran back to the old man. She moistened his face and held his head in her arm. Fortunately, a few moments later two men with a stretcher entered the station, put the man on the stretcher, and took him away. Watching them leave, Mary felt exhausted. At that moment, another train pulled in and Mary, entering one of the cars, continued on her way to work.

Story Three

Joe came home from work earlier than usual, happy that he would be able to spend the whole afternoon and evening with his wife and children. When he reached the porch of his house, he saw his wife talking on the phone in the living room, so he sat on the porch to wait for her to finish her conversation. She came out a few minutes later and told him the phone call was from Tom, whom they had not seen for the last several months. Tom was moving to another city and had called to say good-bye. Joe remembered how two years before when they moved into the city, Tom, who was at that time working in the same company as Joe, helped them move into their house. Although they never became good friends, Joe couldn't forget

Tom's helpfulness and felt indebted to him. Now Tom was moving and probably needed help. Joe decided to call him. Tom said he could hardly manage the packing and indeed needed help. Without hesitation, Joe forgot about his wonderful plans for the afternoon and went to help Tom move.

Story Four

Maureen and Joan, who had not seen each other for three months, were visiting happily in Joan's apartment. After a short conversation, Joan went to prepare coffee. She came back with the cups and saucers and put them down on a small side table. While Joan was looking for a tablecloth, Maureen was wandering around the room looking at the pictures on the walls. Intent on one of the pictures, Maureen took a step back and hit the small table, tipping it over. All the cups and saucers were broken. Maureen felt guilty for her negligence. As she helped Joan clean up, she tried to think of a way to compensate her for the damage. Later, Joan mentioned that she was looking for volunteers to work in a fair she was organizing. Although Maureen had something important to do on that particular Sunday, she decided to cancel her plans and volunteer to help Joan.

DEFINITION OF PROSOCIAL BEHAVIOR

Although each of the four stories involves a different situation, there is a common thread running through them. In each case, one person either helped or did a favor for another person. John gave money to the Salvation Army; Mary helped an old man who had collapsed in a subway car; Joe helped Tom pack for his move; and Maureen volunteered to assist Joan at the fair. Although John, Mary, Joe, and Maureen gave their help because of different intentions, the final outcome of their behavior was the same. Each of them benefited another person without anticipating any reward in return. These types of behavior are called positive forms of social behavior or, in brief, prosocial behavior. This chapter will attempt to clarify the nature and the definition of prosocial behavior.

Daily reports of violence, wars, and crimes have for many years led social scientists to focus their investigations on aggressive behavior. It has become a very important area and social psychologists have proposed theories to explain the determinants and antecedents of aggressive behavior (e.g., Berkowitz, 1962; Buss, 1961; Dollard, Miller, Doob, Mowrer, & Sears, 1939). However, in the last decade, social scientists have become more and more interested in behavior that might be considered the opposite of aggression. This behavior consists of a variety of acts such as helping, aiding, sharing, donating, or assisting. All these acts can be seen as having positive social consequences and, therefore, social psychologists decided to call such acts *prosocial behavior.* Wispé (1972) suggested using this term "to describe behavior which was the antithesis of aggressive behavior, namely, sympathy, altruism, charity, sharing, etc." (p. 3).

This definition raises the question of considering the intentions of the people who help: Is all help considered prosocial behavior? What about a person who helps his neighbors calculating that, as a result of this help, he will be able to ask his neighbor a favor? As mentioned before in the four stories, John, Mary, Joe and Maureen helped other people because of different reasons. While John and Mary helped another person voluntarily and without obligation, Joe and Maureen helped for different reasons. Joe was reciprocating previously received help, and Maureen was compensating Joan for the harm done. Thus, while John and Mary behaved in a way that is considered altruistic, the behavior of Joe and Maureen was a form of restitution.

If prosocial behavior is the antithesis of negative forms of behavior such as aggression, harm, destruction, or selfishness, then prosocial behavior should include the forms of behavior that signify altruism and/or restitution. Specifically, prosocial behavior is defined here as voluntary behavior that is carried out to benefit another without anticipation of external rewards and is performed under two circumstances: (a) the behavior is done for its own end, and (b) the behavior is done as an act of restitution. This definition limits to two types the range of behaviors called prosocial. The first is called altruism and the second restitution.

The definition of prosocial behavior implies that the beneficial act must be carried out voluntarily, not as a result of external threat or enforcement. Prosocial behavior can be carried out only in situations in which the individual has the freedom to decide whether or not to help. It is, however, recognized that an individual may feel an internal pressure or obligation that can lead to prosocial behavior. Empirical studies, however, often cannot distinguish between external and internal pressure. Similarly, investigators cannot determine the anticipation of external rewards; individuals may carry out their prosocial act expecting social approval from their friends or even from strangers. At this time researchers are unable to verify the true feelings and thoughts of the investigated subjects. Therefore, the proposed definition is mostly theoretical, although empirical studies should attempt to control the necessary variables as much as possible. Both types of prosocial behaviors will now be discussed in turn.

Altruism

The first type of prosocial behavior is altruism. Psychologists disagree about the precise definition of altruism although most of them agree that altruistic behavior

1. Must be carried out voluntarily
2. Must aim to benefit another
3. Must be carried out without expectation of a reward (Berkowitz, 1972; Krebs, 1970).

There is disagreement about some specific preconditions for altruistic behavior. Thus, Midlarsky (1968) defined altruism "as a subcategory of aiding, referring to helpful actions which incur some cost to the individual but bring either very little or nothing by way of gain, relative to the magnitude of the investment" (p. 229). Bryan and Test (1967) view altruism as "those acts wherein individuals share or sacrifice a presumed positive reinforcer for no apparent social or material gain" (p. 400). Similarly, Walster and Piliavin (1972) argued that "altruistic behavior is generally thought of as behavior that benefits another rather than the self—as something that is done 'out of the goodness of one's heart' " (p. 166). Other psychologists have stated additional necessary conditions in defining altruism. For Aronfreed (1970) and Cohen (1972) empathy is an essential condition for altruistic behavior. Only help that comes as a result of empathic reaction to another's experience can be called altruistic. Leeds (1963) presented three conditions for altruistic behavior:

1. It must be treated as an end in itself.
2. It must be elicited voluntarily.
3. It must be judged by others as "doing good."

One controversy with regard to the definition of altruism as well as of prosocial behavior surrounds the problem of rewards. While all the definitions agree that a person carrying out an altruistic act should not expect any external rewards, there is disagreement about self-rewards. (Self-rewards are self-administered reinforcements, such as feelings of satisfaction, pride, or joy, as a consequence of a particular act.) Should we call behavior that was self-rewarded altruism? That is, can a person help, feel self-rewarded for this behavior, and still be called an altruist? Rosenhan (1972) and Walster and Piliavin (1972) object to considering self-rewarding help as an altruistic behavior. Rosenhan claims that self-reward is difficult to demonstrate empirically and therefore it becomes a hypothetical construct. Until psychologists can provide empirical evidence for the operation of self-reward, it remains a vague concept. Walster and Piliavin argue that the inclusion of self-reward makes the definition of altruistic behavior tautological. That is, self-reward does not specify in advance what rewards are present, but opens a possibility for circular explanation: Individuals behave altruistically in order to reward themselves or self-reward is only a consequence of altruistic behavior.

The objections raised by Rosenhan and by Walster and Piliavin point out the difficult problem of identifying self-rewards. However it is necessary to distinguish, at least at this time theoretically, between altruistic behavior and any helping acts carried out because of external rewards. Therefore, I propose to limit the scope of altruistic behavior by including only the possibility of self-reward. This possibility was also included in the proposed definition of prosocial behavior.

Thus, in this book, I suggest a definition for altruism based on the one proposed by Macaulay and Berkowitz (1970) with one additional condition. They defined altruism as "behavior carried out to benefit another without anticipation of rewards from external sources" (p. 3). The condition to be added requires that the behavior must be done voluntarily for its own end only. That is, altruistic behavior cannot be carried out as a result of obligation or expectations of quid pro quo. When a person who helps feels that he is expected to do so because of previously received help or because he did harm, he makes restitution but does not carry out an altruistic act.

Restitution

In spite of the fact that some psychologists (e.g., Rosenhan, 1972) identify prosocial behavior with altruism, the definition proposed in this book extends prosocial behavior beyond mere altruistic acts. An altruistic act is only one type of prosocial behavior. The other type consists of an act that aims to make restitution in human relations. This definition includes the behavior of a recipient who tries to reciprocate the previously received help and the behavior of a harm-doer who tries to compensate his victim. However, the definition states that such behaviors must be done voluntarily only for the sake of restitution and without anticipation of external rewards. The psychological basis for making restitution will be discussed in later chapters about reciprocity and compensatory behavior.

RESEARCH ABOUT PROSOCIAL BEHAVIOR

In recent years prosocial behavior has become one of the central areas of social psychology. A formal indication of this trend is the inclusion of a chapter dealing with prosocial behavior in new social psychological textbooks (e.g., Baron, Byrne, & Griffitt, 1974; Berkowitz, 1975; Freedman, Carlsmith, & Sears, 1974; Middlebrook, 1974). Dozens of empirical studies have been carried out to investigate prosocial behavior.

Psychologists have studied prosocial behavior both in the laboratory and in real-life situations (the field). In fact, prosocial behavior is one of the few areas in social psychology where much research has been done in the field. Most of the field studies investigated altruistic behavior; restitution has been investigated mostly in laboratory settings. This is because altruistic studies require only the creation of a situation in which a person would have an opportunity to carry out an altruistic act, whereas the investigation of restitution requires more complicated manipulations. In the latter studies, a person must either receive a favor from another person or harm another person. These are prerequisites for making restitution. Only after these manipulations is it possible to see if the person reciprocates the previously received help or compensates for the previously done harm.

Researchers have designed different ingenious situations in order to study prosocial behavior. In altruistic studies, subjects were placed in situations in which another person was in need of help, and investigators observed the subjects' reactions as to whether or not they would help. For example, in one laboratory situation (Berkowitz & Daniels, 1963, 1964) subjects were playing the role of workers constructing paper boxes under indirect guidance of a peer who was ostensibly playing the role of a supervisor. Each subject was told that the supervisor's likelihood of winning a prize was contingent upon their work output. In another study (Aderman, 1972) subjects were asked to volunteer to participate in an experiment investigating the effects of noxious stimulation. This volunteering did not involve any rewards such as additional credits or money. Subjects in other laboratory studies (Latané & Rodin, 1969; Liebhart, 1972) overheard another person fall and cry out in pain.

In one of the field studies (Wispé & Freshley, 1971) subjects found themselves in a situation where someone's bag of groceries had broken in front of a supermarket. In another field setting (Bickman & Kamzan, 1973; Latané, 1970) passersby in a street were asked minor requests such as directions, change, or a dime. In a third field situation (Piliavin & Piliavin, 1972) subway riders faced a person who collapsed in a moving car.

The experiments to study reciprocating behavior were performed in laboratories. The following examples represent some situations manipulated by experimenters. In one situation (Regan, 1971) subjects received a soft drink from a person and later were asked by that same person to purchase some raffle tickets. In another situation (Greenberg, Block, & Silverman, 1971) subjects were helped to finish their assigned task (i.e., to tie shoe boxes) and later were asked for help from the person who had helped them previously.

Most of the studies investigating compensating behavior were also carried out in laboratories. For example, in one experiment (Freedman, Wallington, & Bless, 1967) subjects were induced to upset a graduate student's pile of arranged index cards and later were asked to volunteer for an experiment run by that student. In another experiment (Carlsmith & Gross, 1969) subjects who played the role of a teacher were instructed to administer an electric shock whenever a learner made a mistake. Later the learner asked each subject to volunteer to telephone people in order to prevent the building of a freeway through the redwood trees in California.

In the next chapters each type of prosocial behavior will be discussed in great detail. However, first it is necessary to analyze how prosocial behavior is acquired in the socialization process. The next chapter will discuss this particular issue.

2

ACQUISITION OF PROSOCIAL BEHAVIOR

In contrast to the extensive research on the prosocial behavior of adults, few studies have investigated the development of prosocial behavior in children. Moreover, most of the developmental studies have investigated only altruistic behavior, disregarding reciprocating and compensatory behavior. The altruistic studies have focused mainly on two types of behaviors: rescue responses (e.g., Staub, 1970b, 1971b) and donation or sharing responses (e.g., Bryan, 1971; Grusec & Skubiski, 1970). In the first type of experiment, the child is exposed to an emergency situation in which somebody is in some sort of distress. In the second type of experiment, the child is provided an opportunity to sacrifice some prized object.

This chapter will review those studies that focused on the processes through which the child acquires prosocial responses. First, however, it is necessary to show that prosocial behavior is learned. The best proof is found in the data that show the relationship of prosocial behavior to age.

PROSOCIAL BEHAVIOR AND AGE

One important finding confirmed by several experiments is that prosocial behavior steadily increases with age during the first ten years of life. In one early study by Ugurel-Semin

11

(1952), children aged 4-16 were asked to divide an uneven number of nuts between themselves and another child. Each child received an uneven number of between five and fifteen nuts. In order to divide the nuts the child had three possibilities: (a) to divide them equally by putting one nut aside, (b) to divide them selfishly by taking the one extra nut for himself, and (c) to divide them altruistically by giving the extra nut to the other child. The results of this study indicated that selfish behavior diminishes with age: while at the age of 4-6, 67 percent of the children were selfish, at the age of 9, only 23 percent of the children were selfish; at the age of 12, selfish behavior completely disappeared. On the other hand, the results showed that altruism steadily increases with age and reaches its peak at the age of 7, when 63 percent of the children shared the nuts altruistically. After the age of 7 the children preferred to share the nuts equally.

In another experiment, Handlon and Gross (1959) investigated the sharing behavior of children in preschool, kindergarten, fourth, fifth, and sixth grades. The children were paired with their classmates of the same sex and played with an apparatus from which pennies fell. When the pennies reached the children, one child was asked to leave the room and the other child was instructed to divide the pennies. The results again showed that as age increases, the subjects kept fewer pennies for themselves. Thus, while the kindergarten children kept for themselves 72 percent of the pennies, sixth-grade children kept only 40 percent and gave 60 percent to the other child.

In a recent experiment, Green and Schneider (1974) investigated age differences in altruistic behavior in three situations. Subjects were 100 boys in four age groups: 5-6 years old, 7-8 years old, 9-10 years old, and 13-14 years old. The boys of the youngest group were tested individually, while the older ones were tested in groups. In the first situation, the subjects were asked to volunteer to put together books for poor children. They were asked to work 15 minutes of their lunch period for either 1, 2, 3, 4, or 5 days. In the second situation, the experimenter "accidentally" dropped five pencils on the floor and the subject had an opportunity to help pick them up. In the third situation, the subjects were given five candy bars and were told that they could share the candy with other children in the school. The results of the study indicated that sharing the candy increased with age, helping to pick up pencils increased until ages 9–10, when virtually all the boys helped, but volunteering to put together books was unrelated with age.

> The failure to find age differences on the volunteering-to-work variable may be due to an inability on the part of the younger Ss to fully appreciate the implication that the expression of intention to help has for their future behavior. (p. 250)

Only a study by Staub (1970b) found that children's attempts to help a distressed child increased from kindergarten to second grade, but then decreased from second to sixth grade. In this study children of kindergarten, first, second, fourth, and sixth grades were taken either individually or in same-sex pairs to the experimental room, where they were instructed to draw something. While the experimenter went to get crayons, the subjects were exposed to a tape-recorded sequence consisting of distress sounds made by a girl who supposedly was playing in the adjoining room. The dependent measure was the subjects' responses to the distress stimuli. The results indicated that in the kindergarten 19 percent of the individual subjects and 50 percent of the pairs attempted to help. In the sixth grade 15 percent of the individual subjects and 31.3 percent of the pairs attempted to help, while in the second grade 51 percent of the individuals and 93 percent of the pairs attempted to help. Staub explained these results by suggesting that while the youngest children still had not learned rules of "proper" behavior, the older children having learned rules of "appropriate" social behavior were inhibited from helping by fear of disapproval for potentially inappropriate conduct. That is,

> one effect of the socialization process is that the child's behavior comes increasingly under the control of norms, either explicit or implicit, which determine what is appropriate behavior in a particular situation. In an unfamiliar environment, when the norms are unclear, he may be unwilling to initiate action, fearing disapproval for possibly inappropriate behavior. If this explanation of the decline in helping with age is correct, it would suggest that the learning of standards of "appropriate" behavior for certain times and places, as part of the

socialization process, may be a factor which negatively influences children's readiness to respond to another's need. (p. 137)

In spite of Staub's findings, the data of other studies (e.g., Midlarsky & Bryan, 1967; Wright, 1942) in general replicated the positive relationship between age and prosocial behavior. Several not-mutually-exclusive explanations can be offered for these results. First, as children grow older their competence in interacting with their environment increases. This competence is expressed in communications skills that make possible complex interexchanges and in frequent interactions with peers and adults. As a result of such maturing, children realize that adults expect children to help when help is needed. This realization may lead to an increase in the feelings of responsibility to help others who are in need. Second, an increase in helping with age may also be expected as a consequence of increase in the capacity to empathize with others, that is, to consider events from another's point of view, and to experience vicariously another's emotion. In fact, Aronfreed (1970) suggested that empathy is a necessary precondition for altruistic behavior, and the ability to emphathize was suggested to be closely related to age (Aronfreed, 1968). Finally, altruism may increase with age through observation of the behavior of adults and older children, through direct tuition, and through reinforcement. It is through these processes that the children may increase their knowledge of how to help others and their feelings of competence to carry out prosocial behavior. In addition to these explanations, from the standpoint of social cognitive development theory, age-related increases in the incidence of prosocial behavior can be linked to changes in the child's moral development. That is, a child's cognitive development is closely related to moral judgment, which in turn affects prosocial behavior.

MORAL DEVELOPMENT AND PROSOCIAL BEHAVIOR

It is possible that older children are more altruistic than younger not only because of the greater opportunity to learn this culturally valued activity, but because they may be shifting the basis of moral judgment from a hedonistic position to one emphasizing social approval. Piaget (1932), the principal proponent of a cognitive-developmental theory of moral judgment, suggested that moral judgments advance in stages related to changes in the child's general cognitive development.

Theories of Moral Development

Piaget proposed the existence of two broad stages of moral development. The child develops in an unvarying sequence from an early stage called *moral realism* to a more mature stage referred to as *autonomous morality*, or as *morality of reciprocity*.

In the first stage the child develops concern and respect for rules. The child feels an obligation to comply with rules because they are coming from external authority and sees any deviation from them as inevitably resulting in punishment. In this stage of moral realism the rightness or wrongness of an act is judged on the basis of the magnitude of its consequences and the extent to which it conforms exactly to established rules. Two important characteristics of this stage contribute to the child's moral judgment. One is his egocentrism, which enables him to subordinate his own experience and perceive situations as others would. The other is his realistic thinking, which leads him to confuse external reality with his own thought processes and subjective experiences. In the stage of moral realism the child initiates prosocial acts only if they are perceived as required by rules of adult authority. Lack of the ability to empathize and egocentrism diminish the possibility of initiating prosocial acts.

In the more advanced stage (autonomous morality) the child realizes that social rules are established and maintained through arbitrary agreements that can be questioned and changed. The child realizes that obedience to authority is neither necessary nor always desirable. The child also learns that violations of rules are not always wrong, nor are they inevitably punished. In the autonomous stage the child starts to judge acts and results of behavior on the basis of perceived intentions. The child also begins to conform more to peer expectations, and he develops the cognitive capacity to recognize and appreciate the needs of others as well as to express gratitude for past affection and favors. Above all, the child acquires the ability to put himself in the place of others. In this second stage, the child moves from an emphasis on "equality," which means that the child feels that all should share exactly equally regardless of specific circumstances, to "equity," which means that the sharing should be tempered by considerations of circumstances. In this stage, once the child has learned the societal prescriptions pertaining to prosocial behavior he is cognitively capable of carrying out prosocial acts. The ability to recognize the needs of others and empathize with them makes the child able to perform altruistic acts. Also, the ability to feel indebtedness for past help or favor and the ability to feel guilt for harm done make the child able to carry out reciprocity or compensatory behaviors.

Although Kohlberg's (1969) theory extended, modified, and refined Piaget's theory, his conceptualization did not change the nature of the relationship between moral development and prosocial behavior. In general, Kohlberg subdivided Piaget's stages into six categories. Each category was based not only upon whether the child chooses an obedient or need-saving act, but also on the reasons and justifications for the choices.

The theories of Piaget and Kohlberg suggest that the development of prosocial behavior is related to the development of moral judgment. Children must reach a certain level of moral development in order to be able to carry out prosocial acts.

The Relationship between Cognitive Development and Altruistic Behavior

Several empirical studies investigated the relationship between cognitive development and altruistic behavior. For example, a study by Rubin and Schneider (1973) investigated the relationship between moral judgment, egocentrism, and altruistic behavior. The experimenters measured separately the communicative egocentrism, moral judgment, and altruistic behavior of 7-year-old children. The altruistic behavior was measured in two different situations. In the first one, the child was asked to donate boxes of candy to a group of poor children. In the second situation, the child had an opportunity to help a younger child put tickets into small piles. The results of this study showed that the number of candy boxes donated to poor children was positively significantly related to both communicative egocentrism, $r = .31$, and moral judgment, $r = .31$. Also the number of ticket piles completed for the younger child was positively significantly related to both egocentrism, $r = .44$, and moral judgment, $r = .40$. These results indicate that the more altruistic behavior the child acquires the better his decentration skills are and the higher the level of moral judgment he is able to make.

Similarly, studies by Emler and Rushton (1974) and Rushton (1975) found that the moral judgment of children was positively related to altruistic behavior. These studies provide evidence that the increase in altruism is paralleled by a decline in egocentrism and the development of higher-level moral judgments related to distributive justice. Thus, according to the cognitive-developmental theory, young children are not altruistic because of their conceptual and cognitive limitations.

SOCIAL LEARNING THEORIES OF PROSOCIAL BEHAVIOR

In contrast to cognitive-developmental theory, which explains the acquisition of prosocial behavior as a result of cognitive and moral development, social learning theories describe the acquisition of prosocial behavior by the same principles used to analyze acquisition of any other aspects of behavior (e.g., Bandura, 1969). That is, it is assumed that prosocial behavior is learned in the same way as any other behavior. Those psychologists who utilize the social learning theory attempt to explain the learning of prosocial behavior mainly through principles of reinforcement and of modeling.

Reinforcement

Social learning theories consider reinforcement to be an important determinant of behavior. The degree of reinforcement associated with the behavior influences whether the behavior will be repeated. Reinforcing consequences serve partly as an unarticulated way of informing performers what they must do in order to gain beneficial results or to avoid punishing ones.

Bandura (1971) summarized the functions of the reinforcements in learning.

> Reinforcements convey information to performers about the types of responses that are appropriate; selective reinforcement directs performers' attention to correlated environmental stimuli that signify probable response consequences; previous reinforcements create expectations that motivate actions designed to secure desired rewards and to avoid injurious outcomes; punishing experiences can endow persons, places, and things with fear-arousing properties that inhibit responsiveness; a given history of positive or negative reinforcement can alter people's self-evaluations in ways that affect their willingness to exhibit behaviors that are discrepant with their self-attitudes and the determination with which they perform them; and finally, the treatment one receives alters liking and respect for the reinforcing agent. (p. 27)

Reinforcements may take many forms varying from objects necessary for physiological survival, such as food and water, to elements of social interaction, such as praise and approval. The former type of reinforcement is considered materilistic and the latter is viewed as social.

Fischer (1963) studied how various reinforcement conditions affect the acquisition of sharing behavior by 4-year-old children. The task consisted of having the children learn to give away at least one of their marbles to children who were shown in pictures. The children were taught during five trials per day, one day a week, under two different reinforcement conditions. Under one condition the children were reinforced socially, that is, they were verbally praised whenever they gave away a marble. Under the second condition, the children were reinforced for sharing behavior with a piece of bubble gum, a material reinforcer. The children were tested for 35 trials, and the acquisition of sharing behavior was defined as giving at least one marble on ten consecutive trials. The results indicated that only 13 out of 24 children reached the acquisition criterion. But the most interesting finding was that 11 children who acquired the sharing behavior were reinforced during the training materially, with bubble gum.

While children in the study of Fischer (1963) were not affected by social reinforcement, children who participated in the experiments by Doland and Adelberg (1967), Bryan, Redfield, and Mader (1971), and Midlarsky, Bryan, and Brickman (1973) demonstrated the influencing strength of social reinforcements upon altruistic behavior. For example, in a study by Doland and Adelberg (1967) nursery children were asked to share pictures of animals with another child. Those children who refused to share the pictures were asked again, this time the experimenter indicating that the child would receive social reinforcement for sharing. The results of this study showed that social reinforcement is an important factor in inducing sharing.

Bandura and Walters (1963) suggested that the effectiveness of different kinds of reinforcers is dependent on such factors as the age, sex, and socioeconomic status of the recipient. Viewed theoretically from the context of social learning theory, it is a possible premise that prosocial behavior is an aspect of the child's behavior that is also learned through social reinforcement. A review by Stevenson (1965) clearly indicates that children's behavior can be effectively affected by social agents, including adults and peers. Therefore, the presence of prosocial behavior in the child's repertoire may imply among other things two possible conclusions: first, that the child is responsive to social reinforcement, and second, that the child has at some time been in the appropriate social learning situation—one in which he has received social reinforcement upon exhibiting prosocial response.

It should be pointed out that traditional theories of reinforcement have been almost entirely concerned with demonstrating how behavior can be regulated by directly experienced consequences arising from external sources. Bandura (1971) has suggested that "out of this circumscribed research interest grew the unfortunate impression that behavior theories view man as a manipulable automaton with hardly any self-regulatory capacities" (p. 20). Social learning theory, while acknowledging the importance of the role played by external reinforcements, suggests a wider range of reinforcement influences. People are not only affected by the experiences created by their actions; they also regulate their behavior to some extent on the basis of observed consequences, as well as consequences they draw for themselves.

Several theorists (Aronfreed, 1968; Rosenhan, 1972) have

argued that the acquisition of altruistic responses requires a history of reinforcement and the development of a self-reward mechanism. These self-administered rewards often are thought to be affective rather than material in nature. The fact that children do maintain certain forms of conduct, without expectation of direct external reinforcement, and sometimes even without the presence of agents of socialization, is a phenomenon of major importance for an understanding of prosocial behavior. It indicates that children are able to monitor their behavior in the absence of control by actual or anticipated external outcomes with immediate consequences for themselves (Aronfreed, 1968).

In this line Rosenhan (1972) suggested that

> to the extent that prosocial behavior involves foregoing rewards for the self while alleviating the distress of others or promoting their gain, it can be argued that something must replace or be more powerful than the reward for the Actor. External consequences are but one of the motivating forces for the Actor. Subjective consequences in the form of affect and/or congition might perhaps be another. In order to forego reward, or to suffer punishment on behalf of another, there must be some amplification of affect for, and cognition about another person or cause. That amplification of affect and cognitive representation of another person, often called empathy or sympathy, is frequently seen as the basis for altruistic acts. (p. 153)

Aronfreed (1970) explained that self-rewarded empathy is acquired through an empathic conditioning procedure, in which the donor's positive affect is conditioned by empathic responses to the recipient's positive reactions to the altruistic act. Thus, the behavior itself is regulated by self-produced consequences of one's own actions. According to Aronfreed, the empathic conditioning is established through two phases. During the first phase the child acquires the capacity for empathic experience which

> consists of the coupling of changes in the child's affectivity to social cues which transmit information about the experience of others. . . . As a result of this temporal contiguity, the cues which transmit the experience of others will acquire their own independent value for the elicitation of changes in the child's affectivity, under conditions where

they are no longer perceived by the child as signals of other events which it will experience directly. (p. 111)

During the second phase of the empathic conditioning the instrumental value of overt acts is established. As Aronfreed formulated it,

> The child often finds the outcome value of overt acts of altruism or sympathy in its empathic experience of the effects of the acts upon others. The empathically reinforcing effects of an altruistic or sympathetic act may take the form of social cues which are directly observable contingent outcomes of the act. Or the effects may have their value transmitted, even when they are not observable, through their cognitive representation by the child. (p. 111)

Empirical support for the importance of positive affect, which functions as self-reinforcement, in eliciting prosocial behavior is sparse, but available. A study by Aronfreed and Paskal (reported by Aronfreed, 1970) is a good example of how children can learn altruistic behavior. In this study, first, 6- to 8-year-old girls observed an adult female operating an apparatus. A movement on one level of the apparatus dispensed a candy and a movement on another level turned on a red light for three seconds. The conditioning process itself was designed in the following way. The experimenter always responded joyfully to the red light: she smiled and shouted happily to transmit expressive cues, and hugged the child to transmit affectional cues. Subsequently the child was instructed to operate the apparatus herself. Whenever the red light appeared the experimenter continued to emit the expressive cues of joy. Thus, the child found herself in a situation in which she had to choose either an act that could bring her candies or an act that could produce pleasurable outcomes for the experimenter. Compared to control children who experienced only the affectional or only the expressive cues, children who experienced both chose to turn on the light more often than they chose to gain candies. Expressive cues from the experimenter served as a subsequent signaling function that the experimenter was experiencing "joy." Affectional cues served to condition that experience of joy in the subject. Each set of cues by themselves had considerably less

effect on the willingness of children to forego their own sweet
rewards than did the combination.

The study by Aronfreed and Paskal indicated that the
altruistic behavior that was finally carried out as a consequence
of self-reward was initially conditioned through vicarious
reinforcement. Bandura (1971) defined vicarious reinforcement
as "a change in the behavior of observers resulting from seeing
the response consequences of others" (p. 24). Thus, in the
experiment of Aronfreed and Paskal the girls decided to activate
the red light after seeing the joyful | responses of the
experimenter.

A study by Bryan (1971) is a direct demonstration of how
changes in the model affectivity, conditioned to the altruistic
behavior itself, establish children's self-sacrificing behavior. First-
and second-grade boys were instructed to play a miniature
bowling game and were told that whenever they obtained 20
points they would receive 3 pennies. The boys were further told
that they could keep the money for themselves and/or donate it
to the March of Dimes. Prior to starting the bowling game the
children were shown a film. In this film a model first received
instructions identical to those given the children in the
experiment. Then the model bowled ten trials, obtaining a
winning score on five of them. On each of the winning trials the
model received 3 cents, of which she donated 2 cents to the
March of Dimes and kept 1 cent for herself. When the model
obtained a winning score she exhorted (only half of) the
subjects to help the sick and poor children. The positive
affective expressions of the model, as a result of the altruistic
act, were emitted either immediately after distributing the
money or after a short delay. After the film presentation, the
subjects were left alone and instructed to bowl and to take their
money.

The results of this study supported Aronfreed's hypothesis
that the model's expressions of positive affect, after carrying out
an altruistic act, served to condition that experience of joy in
the children. As a result of this conditioning the children in
Bryan's study themselves subsequently performed altruistic acts.
However, on the basis of the principle of the gradient of
reinforcement, it was found that children who observed a model

demonstrating an immediate positive affect following an altruistic act were more likely to perform an altruistic act than children who observed a delayed positive affect. This suggests the critical role of temporal contiguity of a positive affect, which functions as a vicarious reinforcement in the acquisition of altruistic behavior.

In principle, Midlarsky and Bryan (1972) replicated Bryan's findings. In this study children were more likely to be generous if they observed an altruistic model who experienced positive affect contiguous to his act than when they observed a selfish model who experienced positive affect noncontiguous to his act. Moreover subjects' subsequent anonymous donations were correlated with the previous training program.

In summary, the reviewed studies clearly indicate that behavior is extensively controlled by its consequences. Responses that produce rewarding outcomes are retained and strengthened. Children acquire prosocial behavior as a result of being rewarded for their acts. The rewards that effect the learning can be material or social. In addition, there is evidence suggesting that vicarious rewards also play an important role in learning prosocial behavior. Through external and vicarious rewards the child acquires the capability of self-rewarding for prosocial acts. Self-rewarding is accepted in the definition of prosocial behavior and therefore the ultimate goal is to teach the child the self-rewarding value of prosocial behavior.

Modeling

Although reinforcement is an important means of shaping social behavior, many social responses are learned merely through observing the behavior of other persons. Especially when novel forms of behavior can be conveyed only by social uses, modeling is an indispensable aspect of learning (Bandura, 1965).

A number of attempts have been made to account for the way in which imitative responses are acquired, and these have been reviewed by Bandura (1965). An early theory of imitation was offered by Miller and Dollard (1941). They suggested that in order for imitative learning to occur observers must be motivated to act, they must be provided with an example of the desired behavior, they must perform responses that match the model, and their imitative behavior must be positively reinforced. Miller and Dollard distinguished between two types of imitation processes. The first type is called *copying*. In copying an individual attempts to imitate another's behavior as closely as possible, because it has cue value to him. The second type is called *matched-dependent behavior*, and it occurs when one individual imitates another because he is rewarded for such imitative behavior through the process of instrumental conditioning. Later Mowrer (1950) suggested that when a model performs an act and at the same time rewards the observer through the process of secondary reinforcement, the model's behavior acquires value for the observer. Under these circumstances the children may imitate adults because this matching of behavior has intrinsic reinforcement value. Lately, Gewirtz and Stingle (1968) and Baer and Sherman (1964) have favored the operant-reinforcement analysis in their explanation of imitation. They proposed that observers imitate because they have previously been reinforced for matching their behavior to that of the model. The matching response itself may acquire secondary reinforcement value. Later through generalization the observer may eventually imitate responses of the model that have not even previously been reinforced. Bandura and his colleagues (Bandura, 1965; Bandura & Walters, 1963) added that imitative learning can take place in the absence of reinforcement. Bandura (1965) explained that "during the period of exposure modeling stimuli elicit in observing subjects configurations and sequences of sensory experiences which, on the basis of past associations, become centrally integrated and structured into perceptual responses" (p. 10). These perceptual responses are central in accounting for observational learning.

Children may learn to carry out prosocial acts through the observation of helping behavior in adults and other children. Observation of prosocial behavior carried out by others may suggest to children that it is appropriate to help and may lead to knowledge of how to help. Children may also learn that helping acts result in beneficial consequences for the recipient of the help, as well as for the helper himself, who may experience the gratitude of others and emotional satisfaction. On the basis of this reasoning, a number of experiments have investigated the impact of behavioral examples upon altruistic responses.

In an early study Rosenhan and White (1967) exposed 120 fourth and fifth graders to an adult model and 10 children were assigned to a no-model control condition. The children in model conditions observed a male graduate student who played a miniature bowling game. The game was played by rolling a marble along a 3-foot ramp. As the marble was rolling, one of four lights behind the plastic numerals 5, 10, 15, and 20 was activated. A game consisted of 20 rolls and the sequence in which the numerals were illuminated was predetermined. When a numeral "20" was illuminated the player won two 5-cent gift certificates. Each child in turn played the game with the model. The model won on Trials 1 and 5 and the subject on Trials 12 and 18. Thus the subject had the opportunity to observe the model who after winning the gift certificates donated half of his prize to an orphan's fund. The results indicated that while 63 percent of the children who observed the model were altruistic, none of the children in the control group donated a prize. For the second phase of the experiment, the subjects were left alone to play one game. Again, 47.5 percent of the children who previously observed the model gave even in the model's absence. Children who did not observe a model again did not donate a prize. Of the subjects who donated, nearly 90 percent had also given previously in the model's presence during the first game. On the basis of these findings, Rosenhan and White postulated that altruistic behavior is derived from internalized norms, which are acquired through observation and that a rehearsal in the presence of a model is necessary in order to establish the habit of altruism. They suggested subjects may assume that their behavior is approved of by the model and that this hypothesized approval compensates for material losses they suffer by sharing.

Contrary to this premise, Grusec and Skubisky (1970) demonstrated that third-grade and fifth-grade children who saw the model share imitated that behavior even though the model was not present and would not know they had done so. In this experiment, children in the third and fifth grades were introduced to a same-sex adult. Half of the subjects then watched the adult play a miniature bowling game (described previously in Rosenhan and White's experiment) and donate half of the won marbles to poor children. The other half of the subjects merely heard the adult verbalize what he thought the appropriate behavior was, that is, to donate half of the winning prize to poor children. Children then played the game alone and the amount of donation was observed through a one-way mirror. A group of control-condition children also played the game without being exposed to an adult. The results of this study showed that all subjects who watched the model donating the marbles shared half of their marbles with poor children. Most of the remaining subjects in the verbalized condition did not differ from the control group that was not exposed to any model and that virtually did not share. The study suggests that the actual performance of sharing by the model is much more effective in producing imitation than mere verbalization of what is the appropriate behavior. In addition, the fact that the children donated without rehearsal in the absence of the model confirms Bandura's (1971) assertion that observational learning can occur without providing reinforcements to the observer. The model was also not rewarded, and thus a child may acquire new forms of behavior merely by observing the actions of the model without experiencing vicarious reinforcement and without overtly emulating the responses while the model is present.

A more recent study by Grusec (1972) replicated some of the findings of Grusec and Skubisky. The 11- and 7-year-old boys and girls imitated the sharing behavior of the model in a situation similar to the one described in Grusec and Skubisky. But the results also indicated that the children, except 7-year-old boys, shared in the verbalized condition (the one in which the adult said what is the appropriate thing to do). Grusec suggested that young girls are more concerned with behaving in ways that would be approved by adults than young boys and therefore young girls followed the instructions of the adult.

Most laboratory studies of altruism and modeling have operationally assumed that altruistic models act consistently, but in real life most children are probably not presented with such models but with examples that are frequently inconsistent. The experiments by Bryan and Walbek (1970a, 1970b) shed light on the impact of a model's inconsistency in preaching and behaving upon altruistic acts of children. In these studies the model preached either charity or greed and later practiced either charity or greed. The results of these studies indicated that only a model's practices influenced a child's behavior. That is, while a behavioral example of an altruistic model influenced children's willingness to contribute their winnings to needy children, preaching failed to increase or decrease contributions. However, both the model's preaching and his behavior affected the child's judgments of the model's attractiveness. That is, the model who preached charity and later practiced it was liked the most.

Other studies (Bryan, et al., 1971; Midlarsky & Bryan, 1972; Rushton, 1975) replicated Bryan and Walbek's findings that behavioral example has an important influence upon altruistic behavior, but these studies also found that charitable preaching was somewhat positively related to the altruistic behavior. On the basis of these findings it is possible to conclude that while verbalizing values may have some effect on children's behavior, behavioral example is a crucial determinant in children's learning of altruistic behavior. The reviewed studies demonstrated that observing others behave in an altruistic manner will elicit altruistic responses from children. If an altruistic child is to be developed, the socializing agent must do more than teach values; he must act in accordance with them. While the behavioral demonstrations provide the necessary information as to why and how to carry out altruistic acts, the verbalized values often do not.

One variable that has been examined frequently in the modeling research is the type of relationship the model has with the child. The model can have a relationship of nurturance or non-nurturance with the observing child; several studies have investigated the influence of nurturance on subsequent modeling. While Rosenhan and White (1967) did not find any effect of nurturance on subsequent modeling, Staub (1970b) and Yarrow, Scott, and Waxler (1973) found that nurturant relations with the model increased helping behavior.

In a study by Staub (1971b), kindergarten children were taken individually to the experimental room. First, each child interacted with the experimenter for about 8 to 10 minutes while playing a bowling game. In the nurturance conditions, the experimenter interacted with the child in a warm and friendly manner, smiling and rewarding the child verbally. In the non-nurturance condition, the experimenter behaved neutrally. Later, in the modeling condition, the experimenter went to an adjoining room supposedly to help a girl who was crying (the crying was prerecorded). Upon returning the experimenter explained that "the girl fell and now she is all right." In the no-modeling condition the experimenter only checked on the girl who was supposedly playing in the adjoining room. In the last part of the experiment, the experimenter left the room and while she was outside the child heard a prerecorded sound of crash and distress from the adjoining room. Altruistic behavior was defined as active attempts to help the girl or to report the accident to the experimenter when she returned later to the room. The results of this study indicated that modeling and nurturance effected helping. While 68.8 percent of children who experienced nurturance and modeling either actively helped or volunteered information, only 25 percent of children who did not experience nurturance or modeling attempted to help. Modeling and nurturance had an independent effect on helping, and both increased helping behavior of the children. Staub suggested that warm, affectionate interaction with an adult may enhance children's feelings of well-being, which may increase the willingness to make sacrifices for the sake of others. More important perhaps, nurturance by an adult may decrease inhibition of helping behavior due to fear of disapproval for possibly inappropriate action. The nurturant behavior of the model may have suggested to the subjects that the model was not punitive and would not punish them for not acting according to the set example.

Modeling influences are not limited to adults or older children. Hartup and Coates (1967) found that children imitate their peers also. In this study, nursery school children exposed to an altruistic peer model displayed significantly more altruism than children who were not exposed to a model.

Modeling and reinforcement are the most powerful socialization techniques; each, however, is effective in a wide variety of circumstances. The experiments by Bryan, et al. (1971) and

Midlarsky et al. (1973) shed some light on the interrelationship between modeling and reinforcement in training altruistic behavior. Both of the experiments showed that social reinforcement effects child's subsequent altruistic behavior. The study by Midlarsky et al. investigated a peculiar situation in which a model first behaved either altruistically or selfishly and later either reinforced or did not reinforce the child's altruistic behavior. The results of this study showed that while approval of altruistic behavior from an altruistic model increased the child's altruistic behavior, such approval from a selfish model decreased the child's altruistic behavior. Midlarsky et al. suggested on the basis of these results that "an adult's inconsistency may cause him to lose the ability to exert positive influence in the domain of moral behavior at issue, or to lose the ability to exercise one of the two most powerful means of socialization, social reinforcement" (pp. 327–328).

While it is apparent that models affect prosocial behavior, several explanations were suggested for the mechanisms that guide observational learning. One popular explanation is that models remind the child of the norms that prescribe prosocial behavior, and thus increase the probability that he will act accordingly (Bryan, 1972). There are data which indicate that children do hold such a norm and do perceive charitable behavior as desirable. Bryan and Walbek (1970b) reported two studies in which third-grade and fourth-grade children were asked in a postexperimental interview whether they thought one should share or whether they thought "children should give their money away to crippled children like in the March of Dimes." Affirmative responses to the first question exceeded 70 percent, while all but three children answered the second question affirmatively. In the same studies children judged the "niceness" of the model on the basis of his verbal and behavioral allegiance to moral standards emphasizing charity. Models who either preached charity or practiced charity were more esteemed than those who simply held a neutral conversation or who had practiced greed. Finally, Bryan and Walbek (1970b) reported a third study that showed that when children were asked to leave a recommendation to another unknown child as whether or not to carry out an altruistic act, the emphasis of the message was upon charity, not greed, even though many subjects had been exposed to a model who preached greed. However, the same studies of Bryan and Walbek have shown that cognitions concerning such responsibilities appear to have no correlation with actually doing altruistic acts. That is, although most of the children recognized their social responsibility to donate, the actual behavior was influenced only by the model's altruistic act. The model's verbal exhortations that aimed at reminding the child about his obligation had little effect on the child's subsequent behavior.

A related explanation revolves around the experimenter's demand characteristics. It suggests that the model simply indicates to the child what the experimenter expects from him (Aronfreed, 1968). However, studies by Bryan and Walbek (1970a) and Harris (1970) suggest that this explanation may be implausible. In the experiment of Harris, experimenters' reinforcement of the model for the altruistic behavior did not affect children's subsequent donations. In the study by Bryan and Walbeck children exposed to a model who was also the experimenter did not donate more than children who were exposed to a model who was not the experimenter.

A third explanation suggests that the model provides the child information about the appropriate behavior to be carried out within the particular situation (Bryan, 1972). Bandura (1971) has pointed out that "a major function of modeling stimuli is to transmit information to observers on how to organize component responses into new patterns of behavior" (p. 10). The child wants to be correct, and he searches for cues as to what is correct and acts accordingly. This explanation emphasizes the importance of situationally specific rules, rather than either abstract values or the operation of very subtle cues.

Finally, Bandura also suggested that modeling may strengthen or weaken responses that children have previously learned. Such learning takes place especially in situations in which the model is rewarded or punished. However, while several studies (e.g., Elliott & Vasta, 1970; Harris, 1970) found that rewarded models were no more effective than models without reward, other studies (e.g., Bryan, 1971) found that the rewarded model effected the child's altruistic behavior more than the nonrewarded model. In the Bryan study, the model was not rewarded by an external agent, but expressed joy after donating behavior. Thus the model showed self-reinforcement. The expression of self-reinforcement on the part of the model was a sufficient condition to teach the children altruistic behavior.

In summary, the reviewed research convincingly suggests that modeling is an important determinant of learning prosocial behavior. Children who have the opportunity to observe a helping model learn what is appropriate to do and how it is possible to carry out the prosocial act. Later, the model reminds the children that the prosocial behavior is the desirable one and strengthens the already existing disposition to carry out prosocial acts.

Other Methods of Teaching Altruistic Behavior

Several studies demonstrated methods of teaching altruistic behavior other than reinforcement and modeling. Staub (1971c) investigated the effect of role playing and induction on children's learning of helping and sharing behavior. That is, whereas role playing involves an enactment of other roles, induction involves explanation of the desirable act and indication of the consequences of this act for the other person. Staub hypothesized that role playing and induction should enhance children's disposition to help. Through role playing, children learn to view events from a variety of points of view. This may increase the capability of role taking and thereby increase the vicarious experience of others' emotions. Staub also expected that induction would increase the understanding of how others feel when they need help and the capacity for empathy with them.

In this study children who were trained to help through role playing were instructed to enact roles in five situations in which one child needed help and another provided it. The five situations were

(a) a child had fallen off a chair in an adjoining room, (b) a child was trying to carry a chair that was too heavy for him, (c) a child was distressed because his building blocks were taken away from him by another child, (d) a child was standing in the path of an oncoming bicycle, and (e) a child had fallen and hurt himself. (p. 808)

The children alternated roles in each situation; thus each child was helping and also was helped. In the induction training the experimenter described the same situations as in the role-playing group and then explained what should be the appropriate helping acts in these situations. In the role playing with induction training the children enacted the roles and the experimenter also pointed out to them the positive consequences of the helping act. The effect of the training was measured in two different situations. In one condition (specific), children were exposed to a situation that was included in the training session. In this situation, children were left alone in the room and then were exposed to a tape-recorded sound of a crash and a distressed voice of a girl. In another condition (generalized), which was different than the training situations, children were exposed to an opportunity to help an experimenter pick up dropped paper clips and were asked to donate received candies to a poor boy. Several days later the children were tested again. This time, the children who had been tested in the specific condition were put in the generalized condition, while those who had been tested in the generalized condition were put in the specific condition. The results showed that following the training in role playing, the girls helped a distressed child significantly more than the control subjects did, who enacted roles unrelated to helping. The boys who had training in role playing shared more candies with the poor child than the control subjects did. Induction did not have any affect on subsequent helping behavior. Also, there was no difference in helping behavior between the immediate testing and the one done several days after the training. Staub explained these results in terms of some sex difference. Girls might feel more empathy to the girl in distress and boys might feel more empathy to the boy in need. In addition it is possible that girls learn earlier than boys to help others in distress while boys learn earlier than girls to share. This study also confirms the findings that verbilization of what is appropriate to do by another person has little effect on children's behavior.

In another experiment, Staub (1970a) found that assignment of responsibility enhanced helping behavior. Children who were told to take charge of things and instructed "if anything happens you take care of it" attempted to help significantly more than children who were not assigned responsibility when they heard prerecorded distressed sound of the girl who "had fallen." Thus the teaching of a norm of social responsibility, that one is supposed to help those who need help, may begin by focusing responsibility on the child externally, by indicating to him that he is expected to respond to another person's need. Initially, children may assume the responsibility because they fear punishment for noncompliance and expect reward for compliance. As time passes, however, through association between others' welfare and their own, they may internalize the desire to help others who are in need.

In another study Staub (1971b) demonstrated that relatively mild experimental manipulations (that is, telling subjects either that they may go into an adjoining room, or that they should not do so, or not providing any information at all about the permissibility of movement) affected the subjects' subsequent attempts to help a distresses person in another room. For seventh-grade children, prohibition and no information were functionally equivalent in their effects on helping, and both resulted in less helping than did permission. Staub argued that the socialization of children in our society may overemphasize the teaching of prohibitions without sufficient emphasis on the norms that prescribe altruistic behavior. The implication of Staub's later experiments is that the children should be explicitly taught to take responsibilities. Such teaching will reduce the fear of disapproval which often probably inhibits active attempts to help another person.

FAMILIAL ANTECEDENTS

The family has an important function in shaping children's behavior. Children's behavior is very influenced by the behavior of their parents and the type of relationship they have with their parents. Several studies have investigated the effect of parent–child relationship on the development of altruistic behavior. In two studies (London, 1970; Rosenhan, 1970) there were interviewed individuals who carried out altruistic acts.

London interviewed 27 individuals who during World War II had rescued Jews. Although the rescuers differed significantly in their background and in the circumstances under which they carried out their rescue acts, all of them risked their lives in some way in order to save the lives of others. As an example London tells about

> a German who devoted himself for almost 4 years to this work at fantastic personal cost and saved about 200 people, [who] reported his initiation into the business with retrospective good humor, as follows: "I was believing in 1942 that the war will be another year. It cannot be any longer. It's impossible. I was then a rich man. I had about 300,000 or 400,000 marks, and I started with one person, then six people, from there to 50, then 100. . . . People came to me—maybe they like my looks—I don't know what it was—asking me very bluntly and very frankly, 'Will you save me?' " It began, for him, when his secretary came to him, said that the Germans were going to kill her Jewish husband, and asked for help. He thought at first that she was crazy, and told her, "Germans don't do things like that!" But she was convinced that they were going to kill all the Jews in town so, although he felt it was not true, he agreed to let her husband stay in his office over the weekend. Through this act of compassion he found himself in the business of rescue. Once he found that the Jews' fears were justified he was pulled in deeper and deeper. (p. 245)

Through the interviews London found that all the rescuers had three things in common. First, almost all the rescuers tended to identify strongly with one of their parents, not necessarily with the same-sex parent. Second, the parent with whom the rescuer identified tended to be a very strong moralist. Such moralism had different bases for different people; for some it was religious moralism, for others it was ideological moralism. Third, most of the rescuers were socially marginal. As an example, London cites the case of the

> Seventh Day Adventist minister from the Netherlands, a country where almost everyone is either Calvinist or Catholic. Seventh Day Adventists

were very marginal socially and not always treated kindly in Holland; his father spent considerable time in jail. Although this minister described himself as mildly anti-Semitic, like his father, during the war he organized a very effective and large-scale operation for rescuing Dutch Jews. The reason he gave for doing so was simply that it was a Christian's duty. (p. 248)

London's findings suggest that a moralistic parent with whom a child identifies serves as a powerful model for altruistic acts. In addition, the experience of social marginality probably sensitizes people to others' needs and aids the development of empathy.

Interestingly, Rosenhan (1970), who interviewed civil rights activists, obtained findings very similar to London's. Thirty-six people who had participated in civil rights activities prior to autumn 1961 provided the data for this study. The activists were divided into two groups: those who remained active in the South for at least one year (fully committed) and those who went on one or two freedom rides (partially committed). The results of the interviews clearly showed that while the fully committed respondents maintained warm and respecting relationships with at least one parent, the partially committed respondents described their parents in more ambivalent terms. Moreover, while the fully committed respondents reported that at least one of their parents was highly moralistic, the partially committed respondents reported ambivalence and confusion concerning their parents' morality. This study confirms London's findings that identification with a moral parent who can provide an example of altruistic acts can be an important determinant of the development of prosocial behavior.

Studies done in a more controlled manner obtained results similar to those of London and Rosenhan. Studies by Rutherford and Mussen (1968), Mussen, Harris, Rutherford, and Keasey (1970), and Hoffman (1975) showed that the affection of parents and their altruistic values are important determinants of children's acquisition of altruistic behavior. Rutherford and Mussen (1968) studied 4-year-old white boys and found that their generosity was related to perceptions of their father as warm, nurturant, and affectionate persons. These results indicate that paternal nurturance serves a double function: it motivates the child to emulate the father's behavior and, at the same time, it provides a model of behavior that is essentially kind and considerate. The father's sympathy and compassion may be conceptualized by the child as generosity. In identifying with the father, he incorporates this characteristic and behaves in generous ways. (p. 762)

Similarly, Mussen et al. (1970) and Hoffman (1975) showed that the acquisition of altruistic behavior depends on the extent to which at least one of the parents can serve as a model for such behaviors. Thus, for example, in Hoffman's study the altruistic behavior of fifth graders, measured by classmates' ratings, was positively related to the same-sex parent's altruistic values. Hoffman argued that

the fact that the parent's altruistic values are associated with altruism in the same-sex child fits well with the general assumption in the literature that identification with the same-sex parents is a significant factor in socialization. (p. 941)

SUMMARY

The findings of the laboratory studies, in which the children were exposed to or reinforced by a stranger, agree with findings of studies that investigated familial antecedents of altruistic behavior. All these studies show that modeling and reinforcement play an important role in learning prosocial behavior. In addition, nurturant relationship with the model was shown to enhance the learning process. On the basis of these findings it is possible to conclude that parents, siblings, and other individuals with whom the child has contact affect a child's prosocial behavior. The nature of the relationship and the extent to which these individuals exemplify altruistic acts determine to a large extent if the child will carry out prosocial behavior. However, it seems that the learning of prosocial behavior can be most effective only when the child has cognitively achieved the stage that enables him to make a proper moral judgment, to empathize with others, and to recognize others needs.

It should be pointed out that the studies that investigated acquisition of prosocial behavior were limited to altruistic behavior. The acquisition of reciprocitating and compensatory behavior has been a relatively neglected area within prosocial behavior. One reason for this neglect is probably the difficulty of staging reciprocity and harm-doing studies in a laboratory.

Another conclusion is that empirical studies have been concerned more with the elicitation of altruistic behavior than with the process by which it is learned. That is, most of the studies attempted to elicit altruistic behavior through reinforcement and modeling but did not investigate the processes themselves.

Finally, few studies have been concerned with the degree to which various measures of altruistic behavior are correlated, and few studies have assessed the impact of determinants of altruism across time or space. Thus, generalization from the findings of one experiment to other behaviors presumably reflecting the same concept, or to the same behavior at a much later date, or to the same behavior in a somewhat different context, cannot be made with assurance.

3

THEORETICAL BASES
OF ALTRUISTIC BEHAVIOR

Why do people help each other, share, or donate? This theoretical question has drawn much attention. In particular, social scientists have been interested in the origins of altruistic behavior because altruism contradicts some old assumptions about human beings held by scholars like Machiavelli, Hobbes, and Freud. Their assumptions state that a person is innately selfish and motivated by self-interest criteria. If their assumptions are true, do individuals help others voluntarily without anticipating any external rewards? Several answers to this question have been offered. And these answers can be classified into four different approaches: the exchange approach, the normative approach, the developmental approach, and the cultural approach.

EXCHANGE APPROACH

Homans (1958), a proponent of the exchange approach, has proposed the fundamental premises of the social exchange analysis of human interaction:

Social behavior is an exchange of goods, material goods but also non-material ones, such as the symbols of approval or prestige. Persons that give much to others try to get much from them, and persons that get much from others are under pressure to give much to them. This process of influence tends to work out an equilibrium to a balance in the exchanges. For a person engaged in exchange, what he gives may be a cost to him, just as what he gets may be a reward, and his behavior changes less as profit, that is, reward less cost, tends to a maximum. Not only does he seek a maximum for himself, but he tries to see to it that no one in his group makes more profit than he does. The cost and the value of what he gives and of what he gets vary with the quantity of what he gives and gets. (p. 606)

According to exchange theorists (Blau, 1964; Homans, 1961; Thibaut & Kelley, 1959) an individual's behavior is guided by the principle of maximizing rewards and minimizing costs in order to obtain the most profitable outcomes in any human interaction. Individuals choose one activity or situation instead of another if the one is more profitable or less costly to them than the other. In line with these principles, social interactions will be repeated only if the participants in that interaction are reinforced as a function of having participated in the relationship. Because the goal of each individual in any social interaction is the maximization of his profits, he thinks primarily of what he can get from others: other people are instrumental to the satisfaction of his wants. The profits include material benefits such as money or goods and social rewards such as approval, recognition, or power. This description portrays a model of an "economic man," that is, one who calculates each act and seeks rewards in each interaction.

According to the exchange approach, altruism is a behavior instrumental in receiving future rewards. Social exchange involves the principle that one who does a favor for another expects future return (Blau, 1964; Gouldner, 1960). We know that those we help are obligated to "pay us back." Gouldner even suggested that there is a norm of reciprocity which "*obliges* the one who has first received a benefit to repay it at some time; it thus provides some realistic grounds for confidence, in the one who first parts with his valuables, that he will be repaid" (p. 177).

Although for many people in many situations externally derived incentives are more important determinants of behavior than are internalized ideals, a profit of interaction does not have to be tangible according to exchange theory. Nonmaterialistic profits such as, for example, social approval, gratitude, or personal obligation are also important "goods" of social interaction. Thus, according to the social exchange approach, altruistic acts may be carried out with expectations of social rewards. Blau (1964) suggested that these expectations are important causes for altruistic behavior.

> An apparent "altruism" pervades social life; people are anxious to benefit one another and to reciprocate for the benefits they receive. But beneath this seeming selflessness an underlying "egoism" can be discovered, the tendency to help others is frequently motivated by the expectation that doing so will bring social rewards. Beyond this self-interested concern with profiting from social associations, however, there is again an "altruistic" element or, at least, one that removes social transactions from simple egoism or psychological hedonism. A basic reward people seek in their associations is social approval, and selfish disregard for others makes it impossible to obtain this important reward. (p. 17)

Homans (1961) went a step further, suggesting that satisfaction of one's values can be an important reward. He argued that "so long as men's values are altruistic, they can take a profit in altruism too. Some of the greatest profiteers we know are altruists" (p. 79). Thus, Homans agreed that doing good to another person may be a payoff by itself. Similarly, Blau (1964) suggested that on rare occasions an individual will help another in need even without expecting any form of gratitude from the recipient. "An individual may also give away money because his conscience demands that he help support the underprivileged and without expecting any form of gratitude from them" (p. 91). Blau considers such an act an exchange of help for the internal approval of the superego. According to Blau these actions are relatively rare. There are people who help others selflessly "without any thought of reward and even without expecting gratitude, but these are virtually saints, and saints are rare" (p. 16).

In general, exchange theorists consider altruism an exceptional, rare behavior. The exchange approach maintains that individuals in most situations help others because they expect material or social rewards. Such help is not considered altruistic, according to the definition of altruistic behavior. The view that people are by nature utilitarian precludes in general the possibility that individuals would carry out altruistic acts. However, the exchange approach does recognize that on rare occasions individuals can help others without expecting external rewards. In these situations, the exchange theorists argue, individuals reward themselves for the carried-out help. As discussed in the first chapter, the definition of altruism recognizes the possiblity of self-rewarding as a result of helping or doing favors. Thus, according to exchange theory, altruistic acts are possible, but they occur very infrequently.

NORMATIVE APPROACH

The normative approach attempts to explain altruistic behavior as being dictated by societal norms. The term *norm* is typically used to refer to a set of expectations members of a group hold concerning how one ought to behave (Homans, 1961; Thibaut & Kelley, 1959). Many norms are stable, because many of the sets of expected behaviors are passed from generation to generation as a part of a culture. Thibaut and Kelley suggest that norms replace interpersonal influence in the control of individuals' behavior. Individuals usually regard norms as rules of behavior and conform to the norms' prescriptions.

There are several reasons why individuals usually conform to these recognized standards of behavior. One important reason for conformity is the concern about reactions of other individuals. A group uses sanctions in order to enforce conformity to its normative standards of behavior. An individual whose behavior departs from the prescribed norms is subject to a negative consequence, which may include disapproval by others. Individuals who follow the norms are socially rewarded by the group. Thus, individuals adhere to the various norms to avoid negative consequences and to receive positive reinforcements. Another reason why people behave according to the prescribed norms is that norms can help define reality and reduce uncertainty (Jones & Gerard, 1967). Faced with an ambiguous situation, people tend to rely on norms that prescribe how to react rather than evaluating the particular situation. Finally, on the basis of Heider's (1958) assumption that people have a need for predictability, the conformity to norms can be seen as deriving from the willingness to live in a world in which the behavior is regulated by rules. In such a world a person knows what to expect and what is expected from him in order to behave in an acceptable way.

Individuals follow the prescription of the norms not only because of external pressure. On the contrary, most of the norms are internalized during the early phases of socialization. The child is taught to behave according to the prescription of norms. Later, he internalizes many of the norms and follows them without any external pressure. On the basis of this assumption individual differences are attributed to differences in the degree to which the relevant norms have been internalized.

Several theorists (e.g., Berkowitz, 1972; Staub, 1972) have suggested that altruistic behavior is also guided by prescriptions of social norms. Specifically, it has been proposed that altruism is regulated by two social norms—the norm of giving and the norm of social responsibility.

Norm of Giving

Leeds (1963) proposed the existence of the *norm of giving*, which states that "one should want to give, not because he may anticipate returns but for its own value" (p. 229). Leeds maintains that the norm of giving is only partially institutionalized. A person who has internalized this norm "has a need-disposition to give." There are three criteria for evaluating whether a person has reacted according to the norm of giving:

1. The helping act must be an end in itself without anticipation of any gains.
2. The helping act must be emitted voluntarily.
3. The helping act must do good.

According to Leeds "the altruist emerges as the pure type who fulfills all three, thus complying with the norm of giving" (p. 231). The norm of giving is usually carried out in situations where there is *role vacuum* and/or *social vacuum*. Role vacuum exists when the norms accompanying a given role do not cover the entire range of possible actions that within normative limits are possible, but not obligatory. Thus, a nurse who takes care of a patient after working hours is an example of one who provides beyond the expectations of role. A social vacuum exists in a situation in which action is required that has not been provided through institutional means or is not capable of immediate mobilization. The natural disaster, an example of a social vacuum situation, provides opportunities for altruistic behavior.

Norm of Social Responsibility

Berkowitz and his associates (Berkowitz & Connor, 1966; Berkowitz & Daniels, 1963; Berkowitz & Friedman, 1967; Goranson & Berkowitz, 1966) suggested the existence of a social responsibility norm, which prescribes that an individual should help those who depend on him and need his assistance. People who internalize the norm of social responsibility "act on behalf of others, not for material gain or social approval, but for their own self-approval, for the self-administered rewards arising from doing what is 'right' " (Goranson & Berkowitz, 1966, p. 228). Thus an individual who learns that somebody is dependent on his help feels an obligation to aid that person, even though he can anticipate no direct return benefits. Although Berkowitz specified the condition for eliciting the altruistic act (the awareness that somebody is dependent on one), he acknowledged, even in his early writing (e.g., Berkowitz & Daniels, 1964), that situational factors may affect socially responsible behavior. In a more recent paper, Berkowitz (1972) stated clearly that

> normative analyses obviously should not be confined to static, internal influences, and must recognize the complex interplay between the individual's previously acquired predispositions and such external factors [situational variables]. (p. 106)

In general, there is common agreement that the altruistic behavior of individuals is not solely determined by the prescription of moral norms. The situational characteristics together with the characteristics of the person interact strongly with the prescription of the norm (e.g., Staub, 1972).

Criticism of the Normative Approach

Normative explanation of altruistic behavior has been criticized on several grounds. Darley and Latané (1970) argued:

1. The use of a variety of norms in order to explain altruistic behavior weakens their explanatory usefulness because any behavior can be described as being normative.
2. Norms often contradict one another and therefore normative explanation is often used as post factum interpretation.
3. Norms are stated too vaguely to guide any concrete act.
4. There is little evidence that individuals think about norms when they behave altruistically.
5. Experimental findings about behavior contradict some of the normative prescriptions.

Krebs (1970) added that normative explanations fall into circular reasoning—tautology—that is, it is always possible to say that the norm guided the behavior if a person behaved according to the norm, and that the norm was not activated in the particular situation if a person did not behave according to the norm. Finally, Staub (1972) pointed out "in most research on normative influence it is assumed that people hold certain expectations of each other, but whether they actually do is not tested" (p. 132).

Personal Norms

As a result of this criticism Schwartz (1973) suggested that altruistic behavior is guided to a large extent by personal norms. Personal norms are defined as the individual's self-expectations which derive from socially shared norms. These norms are products of an interaction between learned expectations of societal norms and personal experience in the socialization process. Whether a person acts according to the norms depends on his awareness of the consequences the act may have for other people, on the extent to which his personal norms correspond to the consequences of the act, and on his feelings of personal responsibility to carry out the act. The personal norms are tied to the person's self-concept. Schwartz proposed that "anticipation or actual violation of the norm result in guilt, self-deprecation, loss of self-esteem; conformity or its anticipation result in pride, enhanced self-esteem, security" (p. 353).

Individual differences in altruistic behavior are the result of differential awareness of consequences and feelings of responsibility experienced by different people. Individual differences in altruistic behavior are also caused by individual calculations of costs involved in violation of the norm in relation to rewards resulting from conformity. The theory of personal norms as formulated by Schwartz makes it possible to test the intervening process of norm activation by measuring the awareness of consequences and the feelings of personal responsibility. Several studies (e.g., Schwartz, 1968, 1970, 1973) have confirmed the hypothesis derived from the theory of personal norms that individuals who are aware of the consequences of their acts and who feel personal responsibility to carry out altruistic acts tend to be more altruistic.

In summary, the normative approach explains altruistic behavior by postulating that many people in our society have acquired norms of conduct to carry out altruistic acts not for tangible gains or social approval, but primarily for approval for themselves. This approach recognizes that, on the one hand, situations are important determinants of altruistic behavior and, on the other, indivuduals differ in the degree to which they internalize norms. Therefore, one individual may behave inconsistently in different situations, and several individuals may behave differently in the same situation.

DEVELOPMENTAL APPROACH

The developmental approach views altruism as a learned behavior, which can be explained within the framework of cognitive development according to the principles of social learning (e.g., Hetherington & Parke, 1975; McCandless & Evans, 1973; Mussen, Conger, & Kagan, 1974). That is, while it is recognized that the cognitive ability to carry out altruistic acts depends on the development of moral judgment and on the capability to empathize with others' needs, one has to learn to be altruistic through the learning opportunities provided by parents, peers, and other adults. In contrast to the normative approach, which analyzes altruistic behavior on the societal level, the developmental approach focuses on the behavior of the individual. Individuals learn to be altruistic and thus the developmental approach says there are large individual differences because individuals differ in their personal experience and in their learning opportunities.

In order to understand the process of learning altruistic behavior, it is necessary to analyze it entirely in terms of external stimulus conditions that initiate the relevant behavior. A number of psychologists (e.g., Aronfreed, 1968; Rosenhan, 1969) have argued that the acquisition of altruistic responses requires a history of reinforcement and the development of a self-reward mechanism. Numerous studies (e.g., Fischer, 1963; Midlarsky, Bryan, & Brickman, 1973) have shown that when helping is rewarded either materially or with social reinforcers the tendency of children to be altruistic in a particular situation increases. An observation of helping behavior is another process through which altruistic behavior can be learned (Hornstein, 1970; Rosenhan, 1972). Several studies (e.g., Bryan & Walbek, 1970b; Hartup & Coates, 1967; Rosenhan & White, 1967) have shown that observation of peer or adult models who are behaving altruistically enhances children's subsequent generosity.

The parents, as primary agents of socialization, are important figures who influence the learning of altruistic behavior. The evidence (e.g., Rosenhan, 1970; Rutherford & Mussen, 1968) suggests that parental warmth and parental moralism are important determinants of the individual's altruistic behavior. For a fuller discussion of the developmental approach, see Chapter 2.

CULTURAL APPROACH

The cultural approach attempts to explain altruism on a societal level, looking for the cultural conditions that may enhance altruistic behavior. One explanation of altruistic behavior, based on biological and social evolution, was proposed by Campbell (1965). He first pointed out that an external threat to the existence of any society or group increases both individuals' hostility toward the threatening outgroup and individuals' solidarity within the group. The solidarity among the members of the group is exhibited through loyalty, cooperation, and altruistic behavior. Individuals are even ready to sacrifice their lives for the group cause in situations of external threat. Campbell suggested that these described reactions have had survival value in the history of human societies or groups. Groups and societies that were able to increase ethnocentric self-sacrificial loyalty have had better chances to survive than have groups who were not able to command such loyalty. Campbell further suggested that "in a long history in which groups and individuals have varied widely and in which only some have survived, the surviving groups will tend to have those social customs and genes which have furthered survival in intergroup conflict" (p. 295). Thus, Campbell premised that the disposition for ethnocentric and altruistic behavior has become inborn as a result of biological and sociocultural evolution.

In a recent paper Campbell (1972) modified his original position proposing that "self-sacrifical dispositions, including especially the willingness to risk death in warfare, are in man a product of a social indoctrination, which is counter to rather than supported by genetically transmitted behavioral dispositions" (p. 23). Campbell's modified theory suggests that altruistic behavior cannot be genetic because inherent in the altruistic behavioral pattern is the very real possibility that the altruist will not survive over the selfish person. In man, genetic competition and selfishness preclude the possibility of evolving genetic altruism. Man can achieve altruistic behavior only through sociocultural evolution, which is carried out through cultural indoctrination.

A very similar view was expressed by Cohen (1972), who agrees with Campbell (1972) that man operates by guidance of self-interest motivation. Altruism is developed only in certain sociocultural reality in which individuals find themselves. Thus, according to Cohen,

The presence and persistence of altruistic values or elements of altruism has survival value for the group that maintains such beliefs. In other words, there is no innate origin of altruism in human nature. Whether or not it exists, and to what extent, lies in the nature and evolution of the socio-cultural system which then has effects on the motivations and behaviors of individuals. (p. 52)

The development of altruism depends on the extent to which individuals acquire feelings of empathy; they can acquire such feelings in social and cultural settings that reward this type of feeling. Cohen argues that the intensity of empathy varies across social groups. The reasons for the differences are the differential family structure and intrafamily relations in different societies. Empathy can develop only in nuclear families that have durable and stable relationships and do not share the household with other adults. Cohen's analysis suggests that altruism can be learned, but its learning can originate only in cultures with certain social structures. Unfortunately, Cohen claims, those structures are not widespread and therefore the emotional components of altruism as psychological attributes of individuals are also not widespread across cultures.

In summary, both Campbell and Cohen suggest that altruism is developed in human groups as a result of certain cultural conditions. Human beings are innately motivated to pursue their own self-interest, but the culture can socialize them to be altruistic.

SUMMARY

It is possible to identify four different approaches that have attempted to explain that individuals behave in a given way because they believe that it is to their advantage to do so. The normative approach has suggested that individuals' behaviors are regulated by norms; the norms prescribe the desired behavior in a particular situation. The developmental approach has maintained that altruism is acquired through the process of social learning and that individuals differ in their altruistic behavior. The cultural approach has argued in favor of the social evolution of altruism.

Each approach seems to present only parts of the explanation concerning the origin of altruism; it is possible to view all the four approaches as complementing each other. Thus, the cultural approach explains how the norms of altruistic behavior have evolved, the normative approach explains the dynamics through which altruistic norms guide behavior, and the developmental approach explains how children learn the norms of altruistic behavior. All these three approaches imply that individuals have to learn altruistic behavior because human beings are innately motivated by self-interest. This statement would probably be agreeable to exchange theorists, who believe that human beings are by nature utilitarian, although they may behave altruistically in rare events.

The next chapter will attempt to explain the variables that affect an individual's decision to carry out an altruistic act in a particular situation.

4

ALTRUISTIC BEHAVIOR IN NONEMERGENCY SITUATIONS

This chapter will present a model that will endeavor to understand the determinants of altruistic acts in nonemergency situations. That is, this chapter will attempt to answer two questions—how a person decides to carry out an altruistic act, and what kind of variables influence the decision. The proposed model deals only with altruistic behavior in nonemergency situations. Emergency and nonemergency situations arouse different psychological and behavioral reactions; therefore each of the situations will be discussed in separate chapters.

The nonemergency situation is characterized in several ways:

1. It does not involve a threat or actual harm to life or property.
2. It is a common event that people face frequently in daily life.
3. It is an unambiguous situation in which the required action is understood immediately by the people involved.
4. It is foreseen and does not require an urgent or immediate action.

People have many opportunities each day to carry out altruistic acts in nonemergency situations. They may be asked by a stranger to donate money to a charitable organization, they may meet an elderly woman who needs help carrying a heavy package, or they may see a person whose groceries have fallen in the street. Each time a person encounters a situation in which an altruistic act is possible, he has to decide whether to help or to ignore the person in need. The model proposed in this chapter analyzes the altruistic decision-making process (whether or not to help), taking into account possible factors that may affect the final decision. The relevant elements of the decision-making process and the factors that affect this process are presented in Figure 1.

The first necessary condition for any altruistic act is awareness that someone needs assistance; the potential helper has to notice that another person needs help. Then, the potential helper has to determine whether or not to help and how to provide that help. These decisions depend on the judgmental process, which consists of two judgments. The first one involves attribution of responsibility, that is, the potential helper judges why the other person is in need or asks for help. The second one involves cost-reward analysis, that is, the potential helper judges how costly in relation to self-rewards it is for him to provide the requested help. This judgmental process is affected by four types of variables: (a) personal variables, which consist of the enduring characteristics of the potential helper such as demographic characteristics and personality traits; (b) situational variables, which consist of characteristics of the particular situation and temporary psychological states of the potential helper; (c) variables that characterize the person in need; and (d) cultural variables, which consist of norms and values that prescribe desirable behavior in the social group of the potential helper. These four types of variables interact in influencing the two judgments. The final decision as to whether or not to carry out the altruistic act and how to carry it out is determined by the result of the judgmental process.

In some nonemergency situations, the decision-making process moves rapidly because individuals face the same situation a number of times and thus become familiar with it. In some situations that occur very frequently, the individuals make decisions impulsively; a person who faces the same situation the fifth or seventh time decides and acts quickly. For example, a

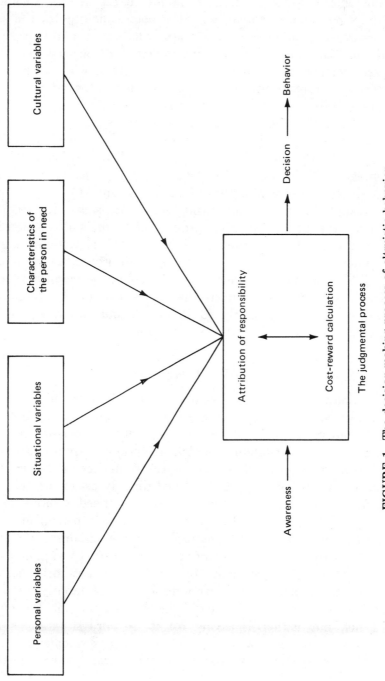

FIGURE 1 The decision-making process of altruistic behavior.

person who is asked to donate money to the March of Dimes by the same elderly woman who has been soliciting for the last ten years, can more readily decide whether or not to give a donation than one who encounters her for the first time. A person facing a new situation or a new person who needs help processes the new information and decides how to act. For example, a person who for the first time sees a teenage boy whose bag of groceries has broken needs to attribute the responsibility and calculate costs-rewards in order to decide whether or not to help collect the spilled groceries. These judgments will be especially affected by the characteristics of the boy and the characteristics of the situation.

Because in many situations different sets of variables influence the decision-making process, it is difficult to predict the behavior of the potential helper. But in spite of some inconsistent findings, it is possible to indicate certain variables that affect altruistic behavior in a predictable manner. These variables will be discussed in the framework of the proposed model, which will be analyzed in detail, and empirical studies will be presented as illustrations for the model.

AWARENESS

An individual must be aware of another's needs in order to carry out altruistic acts. Because nonemergency situations are usually unambiguous and occur frequently, a person has no difficulty in understanding which situations require altruistic behavior. A person can become aware of another's needs in two major ways—by being approached and directly asked for help by someone, or by himself noticing a person in need without being approached directly. In the former situation, a person may be *asked* to donate money for mentally retarded children, to give a dime to a passerby, to help move furniture, or to volunteer to participate in an experiment. In the latter situation, a person may *notice* an old woman carrying a heavy shopping bag or a child trying to cross the street. The old woman and the child need help but neither is asking for it. A third situation is the person in need who passively asks for help. Examples are the hitchhiker who stands by the road, the researcher who puts a note on the bulletin board asking for volunteers to participate in an experiment, and the Salvation Army solicitor who stands with a kettle in front of a supermarket. The basic difference between the passive and the active request is the absence or presence of direct pressure from the person in need.

Although the experiments did not compare the effects of the way in which the potential helper became aware of another's needs, they did manipulate all three types of situations. Thus, for example, in one study subjects were asked by a person whose car had broken down to make a phone call to the garage because he had no more change (Gaertner & Bickman, 1971). In another study subjects were approached in the street and were asked for a dime (Latané, 1970). In these two studies the subjects were directly asked to help. Other studies manipulated the situation in such a way that subjects faced a person in need who did not ask for any help. Thus, for example, in a study by Bryan and Test (1967) a woman was stationed by a car with a flat tire; she did not try to stop any cars. In another manipulated situation subjects found an addressed envelope that contained a man's lost wallet (Hornstein, Fisch, & Holmes, 1968). The researchers also manipulated situations in which a person in need was passively looking for help. For example, in a study by Pomazal and Clore (1973) a hitchhiker waited on a highway to be picked up.

Several studies have investigated the effect of the way a person in need makes a request for help. Thus, experiments by Horowitz (1968) and Jones (1970) have demonstrated that if the request for help is made in such a way that a potential donor does not have the choice of refusing, he feels his freedom of behavior is threatened and therefore he decides to provide less help than when he has a choice of refusing. In addition, a number of studies investigated the effects of semantic variation of help-seeking requests on subsequent altruistic acts. In a study by Kriss, Indenbaum, and Tesch (1974) experimenters playing the role of help seekers called 432 residents of Albany, New York. The caller was ostensibly looking for a garage, saying that his car had broken down. After finding that he ostensibly called a wrong number, he explained that he had no more change with which to make another phone call to the garage, and he made a request in one of three ways. In a negative-toned appeal the caller asked, "Look, think how you would feel if you were in a similar position and you weren't helped. So would you please call my garage for me?" (p. 857). In a positive-toned appeal the caller asked, "If you help me, I'd appreciate it and you'd know that you helped someone out of a really tough spot. So would you please call my garage for me?" (p. 857). Finally, in a simple request condition the caller asked, "Would you please call my garage for me?" (p. 857). After the appeal, if the subject did not hang up immediately, he was told the help seeker's name and location and the telephone number of the garage. A help response was scored only if the subject called the given number and reported the information. The results of this study showed that the positive-toned appeal and the simple request elicited significantly more helping responses than did the negative-toned appeal. This finding suggests that when a person in need arouses positive affect in the potential helper through a positive-toned appeal, he encourages the helping response.

In summary, it is evident that the way a person becomes aware of others' needs is an important determinant of the decision to help or not. Therefore, the effect on altruistic behavior of such variables as the degree to which the help has been requested, tone of the request, and style of the request need to be further investigated.

THE JUDGMENTAL PROCESS

A person who has become aware that *someone* is in need must decide whether to help or not. This decision is made on the basis of two judgments: why the other person is in need, and what are the costs and rewards of carrying out the altruistic act. These two judgments interact, that is, they are done more or less simultaneously and one judgment depends on another. Thus, the person may judge that the other is in need because he is lazy and therefore it is not rewarding to help him. Or the person may judge that it is very costly to help the other in terms of effort and therefore may rationalize that the other is in need because of laziness.

Attribution of Responsibility

Heider (1958) stated that individuals try to explain human behavior by judging what he calls the causal locus of the others' acts or states, that is, attributing causality to others' behaviors. The causal locus according to Heider can be either in the actor or in the environment. Thus, in order to make an attribution of internal (personal) or external (environmental) causes, the perceiver must estimate the relative strengths of the environment and of personal forces. Heider suggested that the most important judgment the person makes is his estimate of the extent to which environmental rather than personal forces are responsible for the other person's actions or state. On the basis of Heider's assumption a considerable amount of research has attempted to study the impact of seeing a person's need for help as caused by internal or external factors. A potential helper judges possible causes that could have brought the person in need to a situation in which he needs help. In particular, he tries to determine to what extent the person in need is responsible for the situation. The decision whether a person is asking for help because of factors beyond his control (external locus of dependency) or because of his own shortcomings (internal locus of dependency) has much effect on altruistic behavior.

A number of studies (e.g., Horowitz, 1968; Schopler & Matthews 1965) have directly manipulated the locus of dependency of the person in need in order to investigate its effect on subsequent help. In one study (Berkowitz, 1969), subjects were ostensibly assigned to supervise the work of two same-sex peers. The subjects were told that the supervisor's task was to write instructions for the workers for making a paper pad and to supply any extra materials needed. They were also told that they could help the workers if they were asked to do so. However, the experimenter indicated that the workers would not find if the supervisor had helped them. (The subjects were told that the worker with the better grade could get a five-dollar gift certificate.) About five minutes after the subjects had provided the necessary instructions, they received a note that had ostensibly been written by the workers. In the external locus of dependency condition, the note said, "The experimenter gave me the wrong paper and now I have fallen behind. It's his fault. Would you please make some pads for me?" (p. 287). In the internal locus of dependency condition the note read, "I took it sort of easy during the 1st period and now I've fallen behind. Would you please make some pads for me?" (p. 287). The results showed that subjects made an average of 7.47 pads for the externally dependent workers (the ones whose dependence resulted from an external cause) and only 5.35 for the internally dependent workers (those dependent by their own fault). Three explanations can be offered for these findings. First, as Berkowitz (1973) proposed, when an individual needs assistance because of internally caused dependency, the potential helper feels a threat to his freedom. The individual in need has improperly imposed himself, and the potential helper tends to resent this obligation. Second, it is possible that a request for help from a person whose dependency is externally caused is seen as more legitimate than a request from a person whose dependency is internally caused. Finally, Schopler and Matthews (1965) suggested that individuals who are dependent because of internal reasons do not sufficiently arouse the norm of social responsibility that prescribes help to dependent others.

It can be concluded that the attribution of responsibility is a crucial judgment, which determines altruistic behavior to a large extent. Individuals who face a person in need attempt to judge whether the dependency was caused by forces beyond his control or by his own fault, and they also judge how rewarding and costly it will be to carry out a particular altruistic act.

Cost-Reward Analysis

The person in a position to help calculates the relationship between possible costs and rewards of the future altruistic act. In particular, the person tries to assess the negative consequences of the altruistic act, such costs as loss of time or required effort. Although by definition altruistic behavior precludes any possibility of expecting external benefits, an individual may expect internal rewards such as pride, enhanced self-esteem, or good feelings. In this vein, Wispé (1972) has commented that "in reality there is no need to argue that an action is less altruistic because the person feels a sense of satisfaction for having done someone some good" (pp. 6-7). The cost-reward judgment consists also of deciding how costly it will be to refuse the request and, to a much lesser extent, how rewarding it will be to refuse it. The costs of refusal include external sanctions such as social disapproval, and internal feelings of shame, dissatisfaction, or lowered self-esteem. Rarely, somebody receives external or internal rewards for refusal to carry out an altruistic act.

The empirical studies of cost-reward analysis (e.g., Gross, Wallston, & Piliavin, 1975; Schaps, 1972; Schopler & Bateson, 1965; Wagner & Wheeler, 1969) have investigated mainly the effect of costs involved in providing help on the decision whether or not to carry out the altruistic act. The results of these studies indicated that help given to a person in need decreased as the costs involved in giving the help rose. For example, in the study by Gross et al. (1975) subjects were asked to volunteer for an experiment. They were told that the experiment would take about 20 minutes and involved filling out a questionnaire. In the high-cost condition the subjects were asked to come to the university in order to fill out the questionnaire; in the low-cost condition the subjects were given stamped envelopes and told that they could fill out the questionnaire at home. The results were that 81 percent of the low-cost-condition subjects agreed to fill out the questionnaire, but only 49 percent of the high-cost-condition subjects agreed to do so. Thus, as Moss and Page (1972) pointed out, there is high likelihood of the "susceptibility of helping behavior to suppression or extinction as a result of experiencing or anticipating negative rewards. It seems likely that individuals may hesitate to offer help because positive rewards are frequently minimal or nonexistent, while aversive consequences for becoming involved and helping are a likelihood" (p. 370). Individuals determine whether to carry out an altruistic act on the basis of judging how much it costs. Most people are reluctant to carry out altruistic acts that involve a high cost.

The judgment of how much cost relative to reward is involved in the helping act and why the person is in need are affected by four types of variables: personal, situational, characteristic of the person in need, and cultural.

PERSONAL VARIABLES

Individuals differ in their social behavior. These differences are at least partially due to individual differences in personal variables, which consist of demographic characteristics and personality traits. Much research has been directed to study the relationship between personal variables and social behavior. Typically the researchers assessed the demographic characteristics, measured different personality traits, and related them to certain social behaviors. Gergen, Gergen, and Meter (1972) pointed out the importance of investigating personal variables by stating that

> In part, the emphasis on personal dispositions stems from the fact that situational studies typically account for relatively small, although significant, amounts of the variance in observed behavior. People import into experimental situations particularized ways of viewing the world, idiosyncratic motives, and varying sensitivities and values. "The situation" is not a constant, but highly dependent on who is viewing it and his particular background. Thus, measures of individual dispositions are utilized in order to reduce error variance and increase the proportion of behavior that can be accounted for systematically. Also of critical significance is the heuristic value of individual difference research. Such study has vital linkages to other domains of inquiry. If achievement motivation is found to be correlated negatively with prosocial behavior in a variety of settings, we have opened a new vista for those whose primary interest is in achievement motivation. . . . In addition, most dispositional variables can subsequently be translated into situational manipulations. If self-esteem or anxiety scores are found related to prosocial acts, it becomes immediately apparent that self-esteem and anxiety would be fruitful to explore as situationally induced states. For these and other reasons, individual dispositions have become an important focus of empirical attention. (pp. 105–106)

Altruistic research attempted to relate different personal variables to altruistic behavior on the assumption that these variables affect the decision whether or not to help other individuals in need. Psychologists have related different personal variables to altruistic acts in order to account for differences among individuals and for behavioral consistencies within one individual. The relationship between personal variables and altruistic behavior will be discussed according to the investigated variables.

Demographic Characteristics

Researchers have studied the relationship between altruistic behavior and sex, race, and age.

Sex

Although a number of studies (e.g., Gruder & Cook, 1971; Thayer, 1973) failed to find sex differences in altruistic behavior, other studies (e.g., Gaertner & Bickman, 1971; Pomazal & Clore, 1973; Wispé & Freshley, 1971) found such differences. A possible explanation for this discrepancy may lie in the nature of the required act of help manipulated in the studies. In the group of studies that found sex differences the altruistic act required either a task usually regarded as masculine, such as calling a garage (Gaertner & Bickman, 1971), or physical help, such as picking up fallen groceries (Wispé & Freshley, 1971); in the group of studies that found no sex differences the altruistic act required was such simple help as stapling questionnaires (Gruder & Cook, 1971) or telephoning someone (Thayer, 1973). Altruistic acts that do not fit the female role or involve physical effort are costly for females to carry out, and therefore they tend to refuse help.

In addition, females more than males tend to refuse help in situations that may be embarrassing or ambiguous (e.g., Latané, 1970; Levy, Lundgren, Ansel, Fell, Fink, & McGrath, 1972; Moss & Page, 1972) because they involve more costs for females than for males. An example of an embarrassing situation can be demonstrated in the manipulation of one condition in the Moss and Page (1972) experiment. In this condition the subject was first scolded while attempting to help, and a few seconds later faced a new situation in which someone had dropped a small bag without noticing it. In this condition females helped less often than males, but in the other conditions that did not involve negative experience there was no difference between males and females on helping behavior.

Schopler and his associates (e.g., Schopler, 1967; Schopler & Bateson, 1965) found that males and females differ in the amount of help they extend to dependent persons. In a series of studies they manipulated the extent to which a person in need was dependent on the potential helper. These studies showed that males tend to help more a person who was low dependent and females tend to help more a person who was high dependent. These findings were explained in terms of traditional sex roles. Males, who are usually highly conscious of their social status, tend to ignore the request of the highly dependent person because the provided help threatens to disrupt their status advantage; under these conditions, providing help is a costly act for them. Females, on the other hand, find a request from a highly dependent person very rewarding because it is consistent with their traditional sex role, which prescribes nurturant, helpful behavior toward a dependent person.

Race

. Several experiments studied the race of the potential helper as a determinant of altruistic behavior. Wispé and Freshley (1971) found no racial differences in helping behavior. Other studies (Gaertner & Bickman, 1971; Thayer, 1973) found that the race of the helper interacted with characteristics of the recipient. The authors suggested that the race of the person in need was the determinant of the altruistic act and not the race of the potential helper. These interaction effects will be discussed later in the chapter.

Age

As was discussed in Chapter 2, there is a relationship between age and altruistic behavior. All the studies that investigated this relationship (e.g., Lowe & Ritchey, 1973; Midlarsky & Bryan, 1967) found that the older the potential helper, the more help he is willing to give.

Personality Traits

On the assumption that some personality traits might be related to altruistic behavior, a number of studies investigated the relationship between particular personality traits and altruistic acts.

Staub and Sherk (1970) investigated the relation between children's need for approval and their sharing behavior. The investigators hypothesized that children with high need for approval would share more than children with low need for approval in order to gain approval and avoid disapproval, but the results of their study did not confirm this hypothesis. Children who scored high on the measure of need for approval shared less candy than children who scored low. The investigators explained this finding by suggesting that children with a strong need for approval may be inhibited and inactive in novel or ambiguous situations because they wish to avoid disapproval.

Similarly, Midlarsky and Bryan (1972) in an attempt to explain individual differences in altruistic behavior measured three personality traits: trust, social responsibility, and social desirability. The results showed that social responsibility, as measured by the Social Responsibility Scale (Harris, 1957), was positively related to donating behavior for girls and boys; the Trust Scale (Hochreich, 1966) was positively related to altruistic behavior only for girls, and the Social Desirability Scale (Crandall, Crandall, & Patkovsky, 1965) had the lowest power prediction. Rutherford and Mussen (1968) asked nursery teachers first to rate the children on the level of their altruism and then to rate each of the altruistic and nonaltruistic children in their class on 21 personality traits. Only on two measures did the altruistic children differ significantly from the nonaltruistic ones. Altruistic children were rated as less gregarious and competitive than the nonaltruistic children.

In a study done with college students, Berkowitz and Daniels (1964) measured individuals' social responsible tendencies with a revised Social Responsibility Scale of Harris (1957). On the assumption that the scale reflects a disposition to conform to the social responsibility norms, the authors correlated the scores of the scale with altruistic behavior. The results showed a positive correlation between helping behavior and scale scores. Similarly, Willis and Goethals (1973), who measured individuals' social responsibility with the Values Scale of Allport, Vernon, and Lindzey (1960), found that while 80 percent of the subjects who were rated high on social responsibility made an altruistic donation, only 42.5 percent of the subjects who were rated low on social responsibility donated.

Sawyer (1966) designed an Altruism Scale that consists of choice items; these items require an individual to rate how much he values his own welfare in relation to others' welfare. This scale was given to college students, and the scoring showed two major findings. First, individuals tended to be more altruistic toward a friend than toward a stranger or an antagonist. Second, students who were trained for social services were more altruistic than social science students or business school students.

Schwartz (1973) suggested that individual differences in altruistic behavior are related to two factors: the individual's tendency to be aware that his actions may have consequences for the welfare of another, and the individual's tendency to deny or to take personal responsibility for his actions. Schwartz (1970) devised two instruments for measuring each of these tendencies: the projective story-completion test for Awareness of Consequences (AC), and a scale with self-descriptive items for Ascription of Responsibility (AR). The scores on AC and AR were found to be positively associated with ratings by peers of the person's considerateness, reliability, and helpfulness.

Gergen et al. (1972) carried out an extensive study to investigate the relationship between ten trait dispositions (abasement, autonomy, change, deference, nurturance, order, self-consistency, self-esteem, sensation seeking, and succorance) and five separate measures of altruistic behavior (help in counseling male high school students, help in counseling female high school students, aid in carrying out a study on deductive thinking, aid in carrying out a study on unusual states of consciousness, and assistance in collating and assembling materials). The investigators correlated each of the ten traits with each of the five altruistic measures. The correlation matrix showed no consistent patterns of relationship, and none of the traits was a good predictor of all the altruistic acts. The investigators summarized the results:

> Thus, rather than finding trait-dimensions that generally predict to prosocial activities, we find that all ten traits utilized in the study can be related to prosocial behavior. However, whether a relationship exists and the nature of this relationship *depends on the type of situation in question.* (p. 116)

These results are not surprising in the light of recent theorizing about the interrelationship between personality traits and situation (e.g., Endler, 1973; Mischel, 1968, 1969, 1971, 1973). Mischel (1968, 1973) pointed out that in recent years a great deal of research has shown that performances which have been thought to be related to personal dispositions are affected by a variety of stimulus conditions and are capable of modification by numerous environmental changes. Most important, Mischel noted that people tend to show a considerable variability in their behavior even across seemingly similar situations. He suggested that behavior is more situation specific than was thought before and "that a person will behave consistently across situations only to the extent that similar behavior leads, or is expected to lead, to similar consequences across those conditions" (Mischel, 1971, p. 74). Knowledge of individual differences alone often tells us little unless it is combined with information about the conditions and situational variables that influence the behavior. In this line, Gergen et al. (1972) suggested that

> what is needed, then, is a trait disposition approach that fully takes into account the nature of the situation and the helping behavior required. The more similar the character of the payoffs from one situation to another, the more likely the same trait disposition will make accurate predictions across situations. By the same token, the extent to which correlations will emerge in prosocial behavior across situations will depend on the similarity among the situations. (p. 118)

Recognizing the importance of the situation, researchers of altruistic behavior have investigated different situations that might affect the decision whether or not to carry out altruistic acts.

SITUATIONAL VARIABLES

Situational variables that may affect altruistic behavior are the characteristics of the situation in which the altruistic behavior occurs, and the temporary psychological states of the potential helper. Although these variables are transitional by nature, because situations are usually not repeated exactly in the same manner, researchers have succeeded in isolating particular situations that have been found to influence altruistic behavior.

Observation of Altruistic Behavior

Individuals may find themselves in situations in which they witness the altruistic behavior of others. A number of studies have shown that the observation of altruistic behavior affects subsequent altruistic acts by the observer. In general these studies have demonstrated that a potential helper will aid more if he first observes a helpful model (e.g., Bryan & Test, 1967; Macaulay, 1970). In an experiment by Bryan and Test (1967), a female college student was standing beside a car with a flat tire. In the no-model condition she was standing alone; in the model condition she was standing beside a male who was changing the tire with his car located nearby. While only 35 cars out of 2,000 stopped when the female was alone, 58 cars out of 2,000 stopped when the model was helping her. This difference was statistically significant. In a second experiment Bryan and Test (1967) found the same results. When a model contributed 5 cents to a Salvation Army kettle, 69 out of 365 individuals also contributed. However, when the model was absent only 43 out of 365 individuals contributed money.

There are several not-mutually-exclusive explanations to account for these findings about the influence of observation of an altruistic model on an observer's behavior:

1. The model sensitizes the observer to the needs of the dependent person.
2. The model calls the attention of the observer to the possibility of carrying out an altruistic act.

3. The model helps the observer choose the proper alternative of behavior, especially in ambiguous situations.
4. The model reminds the observer about the prescriptions of altruistic norms.
5. The model provides information concerning the consequences of altruistic behavior in terms of possible costs and rewards.

The last explanation was investigated by Hornstein et al. (1968), who reasoned that the observer who anticipates having an experience similar to that the model has had as a result of the altruistic act will be more likely to carry out the same behavior if the model has had a positive experience than if he has had a negative experience. However, Hornstein et al. added that the observer anticipates having a similar experience only if the model is similar to the observer. In this study, pedestrians in New York found an addressed, unstamped envelope containing a wallet and a letter to the wallet's owner. The letter was written by a model who had attempted to return the found wallet to its owner but lost it himself. The letter described the model's feelings about returning the wallet. In the negative condition, the model complained that "to take responsibility for the wallet and the necessity to return it is a great inconvenience" but in the positive condition the model wrote that "it is a great pleasure to help somebody...." Of the people who found the positive letter, 70 percent mailed the wallet to the owner with the contents intact; only 10 percent of those who found the negative letter mailed the wallet. These differences were obtained when the letter was written by a model who started the letter, "I found your wallet which I am returning. Everything is here just as I found it." However, when the model's letter was written in poor English, apparently by a foreigner, "I am visit your country finding your ways no familiar and strange . . ." return rates fell an average of 33 percent. These results indicate that in situations in which the observer perceived himself dissimilar to the model, the observer believed that the model's experience does not provide information concerning the consequences of altruistic behavior.

In some situations, the model's act may pose a threat to the observer. If the model carries out an altruistic act and implies that the observer should do the same, then the observer may feel that his behavioral freedom has been restricted; as a result he will be less willing to help. In a study by Willis and Goethals (1973) the model, who was a friend of the observer, either agreed to make the donation in the observer's presence or agreed to make the donation and also suggested that the observer should do likewise. These manipulations showed that the model had a negative effect on the observer's behavior. More subjects donated when there was no model than when there was a model.

A number of studies also investigated the effect of a selfish model—a model who refuses to help—on the observer's behavior. In these studies the subjects were exposed to a confederate who not only did not donate but also made a selfish comment. Macaulay (1970) and Wispé and Freshley (1971) found that exposure to a selfish model induces altruistic behavior. It is possible that the selfish model violates the normative expectations held by the observer, therefore the observer attempts to correct the model's behavior. In addition, the selfish model may, even through refusal, remind the observer about his social obligations.

In summary, the reviewed studies showed that the observation of a person who either helps or does not help affects the altruistic behavior of the observer.

Observation of Harm-doing

A number of studies (e.g., Cialdini, Darby, & Vincent, 1973; Konečni, 1972; Rawlings, 1968; Regan, 1971) have shown that observation of harm-doing may produce an increased inclination to carry out an altruistic act. In one field study by Konečni (1972), pedestrians were exposed to the following situations. On rainy days the passersby encountered a person (an experimenter) who dropped computer-punched cards. In one condition, a confederate bumped into the experimenter, causing the cards to spill out of the folder. The confederate walked away, and the passerby saw the experimenter bending down to collect the cards. In another condition, the experimenter let the cards slip out of a folder about four yards from the passerby. The measure of helping was the number of subjects stopping to help the experimenter pick up the cards: in the first condition, 64 percent of the subjects helped to collect the cards; in the second condition, only 16 percent did so.

Numerous explanations have been offered to account for these findings. These explanations suggested that affective states mediate between the observation of harm-doing and the altruistic act. Rawlings (1970) invoked the notion of "antici- pating guilt." The observation of harm-doing lowered the subjects' threshold for guilt arousal and made them aware of the violation of altruistic norms. Rawlings also suggested that the observation of harm-doing may arouse sympathy, which might heighten sensitivity to others' suffering. Regan (1971) argues that witnessing a transgression violates one's belief that there is justice in the world and motivates one to eliminate the injustice by helping the victim. Cialdini et al. (1973) suggested that viewing harm-doing creates aversive feelings; in order to feel better one engages in altruistic behavior.

These explanations can be interpreted in terms of cost- reward judgment. A person who witnesses a harm being done tends to carry out an altruistic act because, on the one hand, a refusal to help might be costly (violation of one's beliefs and norms) and, on the other hand, the help itself might be rewarding (releasing an empathy and aversive negative feelings). In addition, the decision to help is affected by the judgment of responsibility, which in this situation is attributed to external causes. That is, the observer witnesses that the need of the victim had been caused by factors beyond the victim's control and, therefore, the observer tends to help.

Prior Helping

A number of studies (e.g., Freedman & Fraser, 1966) indicated that compliance with one request increases the likelihood of performing a subsequent favor. Freedman and Fraser called this situation the foot-in-the-door phenomenon, the notion that "once a person has been induced to comply with a small request, he is more likely to comply with a larger demand" (p. 201). In experiments designed to demonstrate this phenomenon, Freedman and Fraser first asked a group of women to answer a few questions about the household products they used. Later, they found those women who agreed to answer the questions were more likely to comply with a larger request to allow a survey team to enumerate and classify all their household products. In a second experiment, suburban homemakers were first asked either to place a small sign in their window or to sign a petition on one of two issues—keeping California beautiful or safe driving. Two weeks later, a different experimenter returned to each home and asked each homemaker to place a large, unattractive billboard promoting auto safety on her front lawn for the following couple of weeks. The results replicated the findings of the first study: subjects who had complied with the small request tended to comply with the large one several weeks later. Freedman and Fraser suggested that the mechanism underlying these increases in compliance is based on a change in the person's self-perception.

> What may occur is a change in the person's feelings about getting involved or about taking action. Once he has agreed to a request, his attitude may change. He may become, in his own eyes, the kind of person who does this sort of thing, who agrees to requests made by strangers, who takes action on things he believes in, who cooperates with good causes. (p. 201)

A study by Schaeffer (1975) provides additional support for the evidence indicating that once an individual has engaged in a prosocial act, he is likely to repeat that act. His experiment found that those subjects who reciprocated the help given them previously were more willing to help again than those subjects who did not reciprocate. One explanation offered by the researcher states that the subjects who had previously helped defined themselves as helpers and were willing to help again.

A number of recent studies (e.g., Kraut, 1973; Pliner, Hart, Kohl, & Saari, 1974; Snyder & Cunningham, 1975; Uranowitz, 1975) replicated the Freedman and Fraser findings and tested the "self-perception" explanation. All these studies concluded that once an individual carries out an altruistic act, he infers that he is generous, and this inferred perception increases the likelihood that he will engage in altruistic behavior later. Harris (1972) offered a somewhat different explanation for the foot-in-the-door phenomenon. She argued that requesting one altruistic act increases the salience of the requirements prescribed by the norm of social responsibility; as a result, individuals are more willing to carry out a second altruistic act. Both of the explanations imply that a person who has helped once finds it more costly to refuse a second time than it would have been the first time. For an individual who perceives himself as generous, a refusal to help damages his self-perception.

Cialdini, Vincent, Lewis, Catalan, Wheeler, and Darby (1975) explored a somewhat different situation. They suggested, on the basis of the foot-in-the-door phenomenon, that first making an extreme request that will be rejected and then making a moderate request should increase compliance with the second request. In the first condition of their experiment, the college student subjects were asked to volunteer to counsel young people at a juvenile detention center for at least two years; when the subjects refused, they were asked to chaperone a group of juvenile delinquents on a two-hour trip to the zoo. In the second condition, the subjects were asked only the second request, and in the third condition, the subjects were asked to comply with either request. The results showed that while none of the subjects complied with the first request (counseling for two years), 50 percent of the subjects complied with the second request in the first condition, 25 percent complied in the second condition, and 16.7 percent complied in the third condition. The researchers explained these results by arguing that the potential helper tends to comply with the small request, after refusing an extreme one, because he perceives the change of request as a concession on the part of the requester. In this situation, the potential helper feels pressure to reciprocate the concession and thus finds it costly to refuse the second request.

Presence of Others

Other researchers investigated the effect of the presence of others when the potential helper is provided with the opportunity to carry out an altruistic act. For example, in a study by Latané (1970), experimenters asked 2,091 passersby in New York City for subway fare. People walking alone were significantly more likely to give the requested money than those walking in pairs or in groups of three. An experiment by Levy et al. (1972) found the same results. The presence of inactive bystanders in the situation requiring an altruistic act increased the tendency not to respond.

Presence of others probably influences the potential helper's judgment of cost-reward and attribution of responsibility. Presence of others reduces the costs of refusal to help because of diffusion of responsibility and blame among bystanders. The potential helper is not the only one to blame for the failure to help (Latané and Darley, 1970). In addition, especially in ambiguous situations, the potential helper depends on the judgments of other individuals present and tends to conform to nonresponding others.

Goodstadt (1971) manipulated a situation in which the presence of others increased the likelihood of a helping act. His experiment showed that if the observer knows that the potential helper dislikes the person in need, then it is costly for him to refuse help. The refusal to help in this situation would reflect badly upon the potential helper, therefore he tends to comply with the request.

Degree of Dependency

The extent to which a person in need is dependent on the potential helper is another situational variable that affects altruistic behavior. Berkowitz and his associates (e.g., Berkowitz and Daniels, 1963, 1964; Goranson & Berkowitz, 1966) were the first to investigate this situation. They designed a standard experimental situation in which one individual is given the opportunity to help another without the prospect of receiving any reward. In essence, their procedure is as follows: the subjects are put to work at a dull task of building paper boxes according to written instructions. Half of them are told that their supervisor, who supposedly has written the instructions and whom they have never met, may have a good chance of winning a prize if they are sufficiently productive (high dependency); the other half are told that the supervisor's rating depends very little upon their level of productivity (low dependency). These experiments found that subjects tend to work more diligently when their supervisor seems to be highly dependent on them. A field study by Bickman and Kamzan (1973) confirmed Berkowitz's findings. In their study, experimenters approached female shoppers in a supermarket asking for 10 cents to buy either a container of milk or a package of cookie dough. While 58 percent of the shoppers helped buy milk (high-need condition), only 36 percent helped buy cookie dough (low-need condition).

These experiments indicate that individuals tend to comply more with the request of a high-dependent person than with the request of a low-dependent person. It is probably more costly to refuse a high-dependent person than a low-dependent person; a refusal to help a high-dependent person may violate the prescriptions of internalized altruistic norms. However, if too much effort is required to help a dependent person, or if other costs that are perceived as too extreme are anticipated, the potential helper may decide to refuse the request. For example, in a study by Pomazal and Clore (1973, Experiment 2), hitchhikers were positioned close to a highway. In the high-dependency condition, the hitchhiker had a 24-inch knee brace on the right leg and a cloth sling on the left arm. In the low-dependency condition, the hitchhiker appeared physically healthy. The results were that the physically disabled hitchhiker was offered a ride by only 16 out of 100 passing cars, while the physically able hitchhiker was offered 34 rides out of 100 passing cars. The passing drivers probably considered it too costly to take the physically disabled hitchhiker, who might cause some inconvenience.

Moods

Several studies have demonstrated that a person's transitional affective states (moods) may affect his willingness to carry out an altruistic act. In two studies, Berkowitz and Connor (1966) and Isen (1970) manipulated the affective state by inducing success and failure. Isen instructed high school teacher subjects to work on tasks that supposedly measured perceptual-motor skills and creativity. The outcomes were manipulated by the experimenter. When they had finished, half the subjects were told that they had succeeded on the tasks and half were told that they had failed. Each subject was given a dollar in change as a participation fee; later they were asked to donate money for building an air-conditioning system in the junior high school building. Those subjects who had "succeeded" donated an average of 46 cents each; those who had "failed" donated an average of 7 cents each. Isen's explanation of these results was that the successful subjects experienced a "warm glow of success," which made them feel more positive toward other people.

Berkowitz (1972) suggested that a pleasant experience

> affects the potential helper's frustration tolerance or willingness to accept restrictions on his freedom of action. He is more tolerant of the demands the help request imposes upon him than he otherwise would be if he is happy, and probably is less accepting of these pressures if he had just had an unpleasant failure. The individual's mood might also affect his empathic capacities. . . . Success might enlarge his ability to empathize with others, while the unhappy failure could conceivably restrict it. (p. 83)

An additional explanation for the success effect was suggested by Isen (1970). She proposed that a successful person may perceive himself as competent, and a competent person feels capable of helping others in need. Kazdin and Bryan (1971) investigated the link between feelings of competence and altruistic behavior. In this study, the subjects were tested on one of two types of tasks: one assessed the physical conditions of the subjects, and the second measured creative ability. Later, the subjects were given feedback about their performance, which indicated that they were either competent or incompetent in the tasks. The dependent variable consisted of donating blood. The results were that irrespective of the nature of the tasks, 26 of the 48 subjects in the high-competence condition volunteered to donate blood, while only 10 of the 48 subjects of the low-competence condition did so.

Other studies that investigated the effect of mood on altruistic behavior manipulated the affective reactions in other ways. Isen and Levin (1972) elicited good feelings in the subjects by giving them cookies. Aderman (1972) manipulated the mood directly by having the subjects read structured sets of elation or depression statements. Rosenhan, Underwood, and Moore (1974) asked the subjects to recall experiences that had made them either happy or sad. All these studies obtained similar results—that in general people in a good mood tend to be more altruistic than people in a bad or neutral mood.

On the basis of the reviewed studies, we conclude that mood may affect the decision of whether or not to help. Feeling good, competent, or successful may increase the self-reward for helping and decrease the cost of not helping; on the other hand, feelings of incompetency, failure, or depression may decrease the cost for not helping and increase the cost for helping.

In summary, we reviewed a number of situational variables that may affect the decision to behave altruistically. (The reviewed variables do not exhaust the list of all possible situations that may influence altruistic acts; only those variables that have been investigated extensively were reviewed.) Several recent studies have added new investigated situations. For example, Barnett and Bryan (1974) found that a competitive atmosphere reduces altruistic behavior. Dovidio and Morris (1975) showed that stressful situations affect willingness to help, and Sherrod and Downs (1974) found that environmental stimulus overload decreases helpful acts. The study of the influence of situational variables on altruistic behavior is in a very early stage, and it is likely that the list of investigated situational variables that affect altruism will grow in the near future.

CHARACTERISTICS OF THE PERSON IN NEED

The decision whether or not to carry out an altruistic act depends on the characteristics of the person in need. The potential helper judges why the requester is in need on the basis of such characteristics as sex, race, or age. Thus, for example, when the person is asked for a dime by someone dressed as a "hippie," he may decide that the requester needs money because he doesn't like to work; as a result, the potential helper may refuse the request. But when a "straight"-dressed requester asks for a dime, the person may decide that the other doesn't have change; therefore he may give it. Characteristics of the recipient may also influence the cost-reward analysis. For example, it is more costly to refuse help to a female than to a male. In the next pages, each of these variables will be discussed in turn.

Sex

Most of the experiments (e.g., Clark, 1974; Latané, 1970; Morgan, 1973; Pomazal & Clore, 1973; West, Whitney, & Schnedler, 1975) found that females are in general helped more than males. For example, in the study by West et al. (1975) a female driver standing behind a car with a raised hood was helped significantly faster than a male driver in the same position behind the same car. This consistent finding can be explained in the following way. The male is less likely to be perceived as being in need because of circumstances beyond his control than is the female; he is more likely to be perceived as possessing the ability necessary to handle the problem. Therefore, the potential negative consequences for not helping him are less severe than they are for not helping a female whose locus of dependence is often perceived as being beyond her control. In addition, the potential cost of helping a female is low because females are perceived as being less likely to harm or to injure one. However, an experiment by Emswiller, Deaux, and Willits (1971) found that females who asked for a dime were less likely to be helped than males. The experimenters explained these surprising results by suggesting that "a woman's begging for money is less acceptable in the more conservative Indiana environment" (p. 290). They found that asking for money was perceived as a male-related behavior and not a desirable behavior in women.

Race

Individuals tend to help others who are similar to them, therefore it is not surprising that the race of the person in need was found to be a determinant of altruistic behavior. Helping a person of the same race as oneself is more rewarding and less costly than helping one of another race. It is also possible that the attribution of responsibility is a function of race. For example, potential white helpers may attribute different causes to a white person being in need than to a black person. In line with this reasoning, West et al. (1975) found that a black driver who had problems with a car was helped faster than a white driver in black neighborhoods, while the white driver was helped faster than the black driver in the white neighborhoods. Similarly, Bryan and Test (1967) showed that black females wearing Salvation Army uniforms got fewer donations from white shoppers than did white females wearing the same uniforms. The latter result was replicated in studies by Gaertner (1973), Gaertner and Bickman (1971), and Penner, Dertke, and Achenbach (1973). Thayer (1973), who manipulated the sex and race of the potential helper and the person in need, found that

(a) When males gave help to individuals of their *own race*, sex was a critical factor—they gave significantly more help to the female than the male. (b) When males gave help to individuals of *other races*, sex was not a critical factor—males and females were helped equally. [But] (a) When females gave help to individuals of their *own race*, sex was not a critical factor. (b) When females gave help to individuals of the *other race*, sex was not a critical factor for white females but was critical for black females. (p. 10)

Age

Tipton and Browning (1972) found that 50- to 60-year-old people who dropped groceries were helped more often than 20- to 30-year-olds. Older individuals are perceived as more dependent and less agile, and therefore would be in greater need of help than are younger individuals; the cost of refusing them is correspondingly greater.

Physical Appearance

A number of experiments have investigated different physical appearance characteristics of the person in need that could affect the decision of the potential helper whether or not to help. For example, a degree of obesity in the person in need was found to influence the amount of received help. Tipton and Browning (1972) found that obese people got more help with fallen groceries than nonobese people did.

Graf and Riddell (1972) and Morgan (1973) found that the length of a male's hair and the type of clothing he wears determine the extent of help he receives. Graf and Riddell positioned a male student beside a car with a raised hood, holding an empty gas can, motioning to each passing motorist in an apparent attempt to get a ride to a gas station. In one condition, the student had shoulder-length hair and wore a gray work shirt, blue jeans, and sandals; in the other condition, he had short hair and wore a sport shirt, neatly pressed slacks, and shined black shoes. For each condition, 800 cars were clocked. Only 14.4 percent stopped for the first student; 20.2 percent stopped for the second, a significant difference. Possibly attitudes and beliefs about individuals who appear to be hippies cause suspicion and fear, which make the help costly. In addition, the physical appearance may also cue the potential helper as to why the requester is in need; one who is dressed sloppily with long hair is perceived as being dependent because of internal reasons.

Similarity between the Potential Helper and the Person in Need

A number of studies (e.g., Baron, 1971; Karabenick, Lerner, & Beecher, 1973; Sole, Marton, & Hornstein, 1975) have shown that individuals tend to help others who are similar to them. In most of these studies the similarity was manipulated in terms of attitudes. Thus, for example, in the study by Karabenick et al., carried out on Election Day 1972, an experimenter who posed as a campaign worker dropped a pile of political placards backing either Nixon or McGovern before a passerby at a polling place. The subjects were interviewed by another experimenter in order to find their voting preference. The results of this study were that "subjects were more likely to help the 'campaign worker' if he had the same political preference as their own" (p. 223). It is more rewarding to help someone similar than someone dissimilar to oneself, especially if we assume that similarity breeds attraction (Byrne, 1971).

Relationship between the Potential Helper
and the Person in Need

In most of the altruistic experiments, the person in need has been a stranger to the potential helper. Nevertheless, it seems possible to hypothesize that the nature of the relationship between the potential helper and the person in need has an effect on the helper's decision to engage in altruistic behavior. In a study about intimate friendship in the Israeli kibbutz and city, Sharabany (1973, 1974) asked 900 children to list names of their six best friends in order. Then each child received a questionnaire which inquired about behaviors such as: giving and helping, imposing and taking, trust and loyalty, etc. The questionnaire was designed to compare children's behavior tendencies toward their best friend with behavior tendencies toward a child listed as sixth on their lists. The results indicated that in general all children reported more tendency to behave altruistically toward their best friend than toward their sixth-best friend. In addition, the results showed that favoring the best friend over the others was greater among children who mutually chose each other as best friend than among children who did not achieve reciprocity in their best friend choices. These results indicate that the more closely the person in need is related to the potential helper, the more rewarding it is for the latter one to extend his help.

CULTURAL VARIABLES

The behavior of an individual in daily encounters is regulated by norms and values that are part of the implicit culture of the society (Krech, Crutchfield, & Ballachey, 1962). Each cultural group has its own norms, which specify the rules of appropriate and inappropriate behavior in different situations, and its own values, which specify what is desirable behavior. Members of the cultural group usually share the same values and follow the prescriptions of the same norms. If individuals behave differently from the prescribed norms, they subject themselves to negative consequences, which may include disapproval by others and feelings of guilt. To avoid these consequences and receive positive reinforcement, individuals tend to adhere to the society's norms.

Altruistic behavior is also regulated to some extent by the values and norms of a given culture. Therefore, we may expect that members of different cultures would differ in their altruistic behavior. Unfortunately there is very little crosscultural research on altruistic behavior, and only a few studies have compared helpful behavior in different cultures.

In one crosscultural study Feldman (1968) examined the differential treatment of foreign and compatriot strangers by Parisians, Athenians, and Bostonians in different social contexts. In one situation, passersby in the three cities were asked directions by a compatriot couple and by a foreign couple. In a second situation, male passersby were asked by a male compatriot or foreigner to mail a letter that was either stamped or unstamped. The subjects reacted somewhat differently in the two situations. In the first situation, Parisians and Athenians helped the compatriot more often than they did the foreigner; Bostonians did not differ in their help to the compatriot and to the foreigner. In general, the Bostonians were the most helpful to the compatriot and to the foreigner. The Parisians were the least helpful to the foreigner, and the Athenians were the least helpful to the compatriot. In the second situation, Athenians treated the compatriot worse than they did the foreigner; Bostonians treated the foreigner worse than they did the compatriot; and Parisians treated the foreigner and the compatriot the same. In general, Parisians treated the foreigner the best, and no difference was found between the treatment of the foreigner in Athens and the treatment in Boston. Athenians treated the compatriot the worst, and Bostonians and Parisians treated the compatriot the same. These results indicated that although members of different cultures differ in their altruistic behavior, their acts are determined to a large extent by the specific conditions of a situation. As a result, any firm conclusions about cultural differences in this study cannot be drawn.

In another study, Berkowitz (1966) compared altruistic behavior of boys from Madison, Wisconsin, with altruistic behavior of boys from Oxford, England. The American boys were recruited from three different socioeconomic classes: the bureaucratic middle class (who work for someone else), the entrepreneurial middle class (whose income is determined by their own action), and the working class. The English boys came from the bureaucratic middle class and the working class. In both cities, the experiment was carried out in two phases. In the first phase, each boy was instructed to write a note to another boy (who actually did not exist) in the other room, explaining how to perform a certain task. The subject was told that he could win a cash prize if he gave a good explanation, but that his prize depended to a large extent upon another boy's productivity. Later, half the subjects were told that the other boy had worked hard helping them to get the prize, and half were told that the other boy had not worked hard. In the second phase, the roles were reversed; each boy was performing supposedly under the instructions of the other boy, whose prize was now supposedly dependent on the subjects' productivity. Half the subjects were told that they would work with the same boy who had previously been their supervisor, and half were told that they would work for a different boy. The results of this study showed similar behavior of American and English boys. In both places, bureaucratic middle-class boys were in general the most helpful, disregarding the level of help they had received earlier. The American boys from the entrepreneurial middle class and the English boys from the working class were helpful only to boys from whom they had previously gotten help.

In a recent study L'Armand and Pepitone (1975) compared altruistic behavior in India and the United States. This study showed that in general American subjects were more altruistic than Indian subjects. However, the altruism of the Americans was limited to situations in which no cost was involved in being altruistic. In a competitive situation in which subjects' losses were in proportion to others' gains, the altruistic behavior tended to vanish. L'Armand and Pepitone explained the low level of altruistic behavior by Indian subjects by suggesting that individuals in underdeveloped societies, such as India, believe that all types of rewards in the world are fixed and severely limited. Moreover, a gain by one person causes a loss to another.

Thus, individuals who hold such beliefs will not tend to be altruistic.

Krech et al. (1962) noted that a complex society has "a number of subcultures or part-cultures with more or less characteristic and distinctive designs for living" (p. 372). The major subcultures are based on social class and ethnic differences. A number of studies compared the altruistic behavior of different socioeconomic classes.

In this vein, Muir and Weinstein (1962) reported that in the United States, upper-middle-class females tend to deal with other people according to exchange principles. They tend to cut off help from people who failed to repay their debts and felt especially obligated to do favors for people who had helped them in the past. On the other hand, lower-class females tended to help when they were able. The investigators concluded that members of the lower class tend to extend to each other "mutual aid . . . especially since exchanges appeared to be family centered" (p. 538). Members of the middle class are guided by reciprocity principles paralleled to financial exchanges that characterize business transactions.

A somewhat similar result was found in other countries. In Turkey, Ugurel-Semin (1952) found that lower-class children shared less than middle-class children. In Israel, Dreman and Greenbaum (1973) found that middle-class children, particularly males, tend to rely on reciprocity principles in their donations.

Berkowitz and Friedman (1967), in a study described previously by Berkowitz (1966), inquired further into the altruistic behavior of middle-class individuals. They suggested a distinction between those middle-class members who are entrepreneurs and those who are bureaucrats. While entrepreneurs should be guided by exchange principles, the bureaucrats should adhere to altruistic norms. Their experiment compared helping behavior of boys from different social classes, and the results showed that the boys from entrepreneurial middle-class families tended to help only to the extent that they had received previous help. Boys from bureaucratic middle-class and working-class families helped without considering prior help.

A study by Sharabany (1973, 1974) compared reported altruistic behavior between children who live in an agricultural-communal settlement and children who live in cities. The comparison indicated that altruistic behavior between intimate friends was greater in the city than in the kibbutz. One possible interpretation offered by the researcher is that in the kibbutz, dyadic intimate relations are less intensive than in the city because of the group upbringing, which simultaneously discourages dyadic relations and encourages reliance on all the group members.

SUMMARY

The proposed model takes into account the four explanations of altruistic behavior presented in Chapter 3. The model takes into consideration the individual's cost-reward calculation as suggested by the exchange approach, and it recognizes individual and cultural differences as suggested by the normative, motivational, and cultural approaches. All these factors are included in the potential helper's decision-making process. This process consists of two basic judgments: why the other person is in need, and how costly and rewarding it will be to carry out the altruistic act. This cognitive process is affected by four types of variables: personal, situational, characteristics of the person in need, and cultural. This model is limited to altruistic behavior in nonemergency situations. The next chapter will discuss altruistic behavior in emergency situations.

5

ALTRUISTIC BEHAVIOR IN EMERGENCY SITUATIONS

On March 14, 1964, a story detailing a crime appeared in the *New York Times*. The crime was the murder of a New York City woman by the name of Catherine Genovese.

This could have been one of hundreds of murder stories that appear each year in different newspapers, but the story of Kitty Genovese turned into an important landmark in social psychological research. There have been few real-life events that have stimulated so much research as the case of Kitty Genovese. The reason for this development was the discovery during the investigation of the fact that, as Kitty Genovese was being murdered, 38 of her neighbors watched the tragedy. A. M. Rosenthal, the metropolitan editor of the *New York Times*, accidentally discovered the existence of these witnesses and described the event in his book, *Thirty-Eight Witnesses*:

> On the night of March 13, about 3 a.m., Catherine Genovese was returning to her home. She worked late as manager of a bar in Hollis, another part of Queens. She parked her car (a red Fiat) and started to walk to her death.
>
> Lurking near the parking lot was a man. Miss Genovese saw him in the shadows, turned and walked toward a police call box. The man pursued her, stabbed her. She screamed, "Oh my God, he stabbed me! Please help me! Please help me!"

Somebody threw open a window and a man called out: "Let that girl alone!" Other lights turned on, other windows were raised. The attacker got into a car and drove away. A bus passed.

The attacker drove back, got out, searched out Miss Genovese in the back of an apartment building where she had crawled for safety, stabbed her again, drove away again.

The first attack came at 3:15. The first call to the police came at 3:50. Police arrived within two minutes, they say. Miss Genovese was dead.

That night and the next morning the police combed the neighborhood looking for witnesses. They found them, 38.

Two weeks later, when this newspaper [the *New York Times*] heard of the story, a reporter went knocking door to door, asking why, why.

Through half-opened doors, they told him. Most of them were neither defiant nor terribly embarrassed nor particularly ashamed. The underlying attitude, or explanation, seemed to be fear of involvement— any kind of involvement.

"I didn't want my husband to get involved," a housewife said.

"We thought it was a lovers' quarrel," said another woman, "I went back to bed."

"I was tired," said a man.

"I don't know," said another man.

"I don't know," said still another.

"I don't know," said others. (Rosenthal, 1964, pp. 78–79)

Two social psychologists, John Darley and Bibb Latané, became interested in the case, particularly in this question: Why did nobody intervene? With the publicity given to the Genovese case, general interest in altruism has increased, and the question of how, why, and whether people help in emergencies had emerged as a central area of social psychology. In recent years, social psychologists (e.g., Latané & Darley, 1968; Latané & Rodin, 1969; Piliavin, Rodin, & Piliavin, 1969; Suedfeld, Bochner, & Wnek, 1972) have investigated the phenomenon of helping in emergencies by simulating emergency situations and observing individuals' reactions. Such experiments have been carried out in both laboratory and field settings and have investigated mainly the situational and personal variables of the potential helper that may increase or decrease the likelihood of intervention.

This chapter will discuss the proposed models of helping in

emergency situations, review the empirical research, and finally suggest a new model of intervention.

WHAT IS AN EMERGENCY SITUATION?

First of all, it is necessary to define what is meant by an emergency situation. Latané and Darley (1970) said the emergency situation has five distinctive characteristics:

1. It "involves threat of harm or actual harm to life or property" (accidents, fires, floods are only some examples of emergency situations); because of the danger intervention in an emergency situation can be very costly, and in some cases the helper may even be in danger.
2. It is an "unusual and rare event." People (except those in particular professions) face very few emergency situations in their lives; most individuals who are thrown into emergencies have little or no experience in handling such situations.
3. The emergency situation is unique; each situation presents a specific problem, each requires a unique type of intervention, and each demands the helper to have different skills. For example, while a drowning accident requires swimming skills and knowledge of artificial respiration techniques, a fire in a house requires knowing where to find a phone and how to extinguish burning materials.
4. Emergency situations are usually unforeseen and unpredictable; as a result it is impossible to plan any intervention in advance. Nobody can know how, where, and when the emergency will occur, and when an emergency does occur, the individuals involved are often unprepared to handle it. (There are, however, a few emergencies that can be predicted; under certain circumstances, such emergencies as floods or volcanic eruption can be predicted.)
5. The emergency situation requires immediate intervention; a delay may result in tragic consequences. The potential

helper is under pressure to act immediately, before the situation deteriorates.

In addition to the five characteristics Latané and Darley listed, Piliavin and Piliavin (1972) suggested that emergency situations elicit a state of physiological arousal.

Finally, emergency situations can be characterized by the nature of possible interventions. Helping in emergency situations can be done in two ways—direct and indirect. Direct help occurs when the helper himself actually steps into the situation, trying to save the victim or the property; catching a thief, putting out a fire, taking an injured person to a hospital are examples of direct intervention. Indirect intervention involves telling somebody qualified to handle an emergency about it; a person may call the police, the fire department, or a doctor.

A number of psychologists have proposed decision-making models that explain the mental process of the potential helper in an emergency situation. Such models make it possible to understand what determines whether or not a bystander will intervene to help. One of the first models was proposed by Latané and Darley (1970).

LATANÉ AND DARLEY'S APPROACH

Latané and Darley (1970), pioneers in research on emergency help, suggested a theoretical framework for their research and performed a number of empirical studies.

The Decision-making Model

Latané and Darley's model of the helping process for emergency situations consists of five decisions in a sequence. However, the decision maker may cycle back and forth in the stages of decisions; the decision made may be reconsidered again in the further stages of the process. The five decisions follow.

First, "a person must notice that something is happening." Individuals are usually absorbed with their own thoughts and deeds, rushing to meet their own goals, and often may not even notice emergency situations happening around them.

If however a person notices that something is happening, then, second, he must decide whether the event is an emergency or not. Emergency situations are rare, sometimes ambiguous, events, and a person may have difficulty interpreting what has happened. It may be difficult to decide for example whether a person lying in the street is drunk, sick, or homeless. For convenience, a person may also distort his perception, convincing himself that a situation does not involve an emergency; it is easier to decide that the witnessed beating is part of a lovers' quarrel than an attempted rape. The interpretation of the nature of the event depends on several variables such as past experience and the reaction of other bystanders.

A third decision a bystander faces, if he has noticed the event and identified it as an emergency, is whether he has personal responsibility to help, whether to involve himself in the situation and intervene. This is a crucial decision. It is often simpler to decide that "it is not my business" than to get involved and incur possible costs. Many different variables may influence the individual's decision to assume personal responsibility; the potential helper's competence, sex, age, social role, and relationship with the victim, and the victim's sex, age, and race are only some examples of possible variables.

The fourth decision is how to intervene and what mode of help to use. The two alternatives are indirect and direct help. Once one of the alternatives has been decided on, the potential helper must decide what to do. Indirect help may consist of phoning the police, shouting for help, or knocking on a neighbor's door. When deciding on direct help, he chooses a course of intervention under great pressure.

The last decision a person in an emergency situation must make is how to implement the fourth decision. At this point, the potential helper starts to carry out the intervention.

In order to study the variables that affect the proposed decision-making process, Darley and Latané developed three paradigms. These paradigms involved three different manipulated emergency situations that were later modeled by other social psychologists (e.g., Bickman, 1971; Clark & Word, 1972; Liebhart, 1972; Ross & Braband, 1973; Smith, Smythe, & Lien,

1972). The three situations were manipulated in a laboratory, and college students served as subjects.

Situation One: Smoke in the Room

In the first situation the subjects were invited by telephone to volunteer to be interviewed about problems of urban life (Latané & Darley, 1968). When they came to the appointed room, they found a large sign on the wall that requested them to wait for the interviewer and while waiting to fill out a preliminary questionnaire. The subjects usually followed the instructions and started to fill out the questionnaire. After they had been writing for several minutes, smoke began to pour into the room through a small vent in the wall. The smoke continued until, by the end of four minutes, it had filled the whole room sufficiently to produce a mildly acrid odor and to interfere with the vision and breathing of the subjects. The subjects' behavior was observed through a one-way mirror. If nobody reported the smoke in six minutes from the time it was noticed, the experiment was terminated.

Situation Two: Epileptic Seizure

In another experiment by Darley and Latané (1968) each subject was brought to a small room and fitted with a pair of headphones attached to a microphone. The experimenter made the subject think that several other subjects were participating in the experiment. Over the intercom, the experimenter explained that the research involved discussion about personal problems that college students face in an urban environment and that communication would be by intercom in order to avoid embarrassment and to preserve anonymity. The experimenter also announced that he would not listen to the discussion in order not to inhibit it. He then instructed the subjects to talk in turn for about two minutes. In order to control the time, each microphone was activated for only two minutes; only one subject could be heard at any given time. In fact, all the voices except the subjects' were prerecorded. The first recorded "subject" (a future "victim") spoke hesitantly of his proneness to seizures. The other "subjects" discussed other problems, and the real subject spoke last. When the "victim's" turn came again to speak, he made some comments and then suddenly started to mumble:

> I er I think I I need er if if could er er somebody er er er er er er er give me a little er give me a little help here because I er I'm er er h-h-having a a a a real problem er right now and I er if somebody could help me out it would er er s-s-sure be sure be good . . . because er there er er a cause I er I uh I've got a a one of the er sie . . . er er things coming on and and and I could really er use some help so if somebody would er give me a little h-help uh er er er er er c-could somebody er er help uh uh uh (*choking sounds*). . . . I'm gonna die er er I'm . . . gonna er help er er seizure (*chokes, then quiet*).

The victim's speech continued for about 125 seconds and then was cut off.

Situation Three: Injured Woman

In the third situation (Latané & Rodin, 1969), the subjects were asked by telephone to participate in a Consumer Testing Bureau survey concerning games and puzzles preferences. When the subjects arrived, either in pairs or alone, they were met by a woman posing as a market research representative. On the way to the testing room she took them past her office, which was separated from the testing room by a collapsible curtain; she made sure they understood that the curtain was unlocked. In the testing room, the woman asked the subjects to fill out some preliminary questionnaires and went into her office, where for four minutes she made noise by opening and closing drawers and then turned on a tape recorder that played a tape of her climbing up on a chair, a loud crash, and a scream, "Oh, my God, my foot . . . I . . . I . . . can't move it. Oh . . . my ankle . . . I . . . can't get this . . . thing . . . off me" (p. 192). She moaned for about 60 seconds and gradually started to calm. After 130 seconds, she got up and left the room.

Findings

The major focus in these three experiments was the examination of the relationship between the number of bystanders and the likelihood that the bystander would intervene in the emergency. The results obtained consistently in all three experiments were that the likelihood that any given bystander would intervene in an emergency decreased as the number of bystanders present increased. As Latané and Darley (1970) said,

> In general, we suggest, factors affecting the process by which an individual interprets an emergency may be more important determinants of his action than his general motivation to help others. Specifically, we think that the number of other people present at an emergency may have important effects on whether any individual will intervene. (p. 42)

Latané and Darley later replicated their findings while manipulating additional variables such as the sex of the bystanders, relationship among bystanders, acquaintanceship of the bystanders with the victim, competence of the bystanders, and age of the bystanders. In all these experiments, the number of bystanders present in the emergency situation was always the most critical variable that determined the likelihood of helping behavior. The presence of fellow bystanders had an inhibiting effect on the intervention. Latané and Darley (1970) offered a number of explanations for this effect:

1. The individual calculates his behavior very carefully whenever other individuals are present; he tries to avoid an action that may embarrass him in the presence of others. In an emergency situation the helper may find himself ridiculed (for example, where a person lying on the street is drunk, not sick as the helper had thought); therefore the presence of others inhibits his possible intervention.
2. Individuals tend to model the behavior of others. If other bystanders do not intervene in an emergency situation, the potential helper may conform, and together with others will remain inactive.
3. The presence of other people affects one's perception of a situation and makes it seem less critical.

Latané and Darley (1970) called such indifference "pluralistic ignorance," which develops when "each person decides that since nobody is concerned, nothing is wrong."

4. When other individuals are present, the cost of not helping decreases; the possible feelings of guilt, shame, or blame are diffused among the bystanders.

Latané and Darley (1970) called this phenomenon "diffusion of responsibility":

> If only one bystander is present at an emergency, he carries all of the responsibility for dealing with it; he will feel all of the guilt for not acting; he will bear all of the blame that accrues for nonintervention. If others are present, the onus of responsibility is diffused, and the finger of blame points less directly at any one person. The individual may be more likely to resolve his conflict between intervening and nonintervening in favor of the latter alternative. (p. 90)

It should be noted that the Latané and Darley experiments were carried out in laboratory settings. These laboratory experiments, which simulated real-life emergencies, are different from the real-life situations. Latané and Darley (1970) themselves criticized the shortcomings of their laboratory experiments. "A major difficulty with laboratory studies of helping is that they are hard to relate to real-life situations" (p. 7).

Subjects who faced the emergency situation knew that they were participating in an experiment. There is evidence (e.g., Orne & Evans, 1965) that subjects in a laboratory experiment give themselves into the experimenter's hand; whatever happens in the experiment is the experimenter's responsibility, not theirs.

In addition, Latané and Darley's experiments were set up in such a way that the subjects could not see the accident or the victim. Such manipulations could reduce the impact of the emergency. It is, therefore, not surprising that two field studies (Piliavin & Piliavin, 1972; Piliavin et al., 1969) did not find the "diffusion of responsibility effect." In order to account for these results the Piliavins proposed a two-phase model of bystander reaction.

PILIAVIN AND PILIAVIN'S APPROACH

The model of Piliavin and Piliavin (see Piliavin & Piliavin, 1972; Piliavin et al., 1969) assumes that observation of an emergency situation elicits a state of physiological arousal in the bystander. The feeling of arousal is the first phase in the bystander's reaction to an emergency situation. The degree of arousal he experiences depends on a number of variables:

1. Perceived severity of the emergency situation: the greater the severity the higher the arousal
2. Physical distance from the emergency: the closer the bystander is to the emergency the higher the arousal
3. Feelings of empathy: if the bystander feels empathy as a result of perceived similarity to the victim or emotional attachment to the victim, then he will experience a high level of arousal
4. Length of the emergency: the longer the emergency lasts without any help, the higher the arousal

Further, the model postulates that the arousal is aversive and the bystander is therefore motivated to reduce or eliminate it. Reduction of the arousal can be done in one of a number of possible ways: a person may intervene directly by stepping into the emergency scene, intervene indirectly by notifying the relevant authority or someone else about the emergency, leave the scene of the emergency without doing anything, or stay watching without intervening. The Piliavins suggested that the choice of a particular action depends on the cost and rewards involved in helping and not helping. A person calculates the costs and rewards and then decides what to do:

> The response that will be chosen is a function of a cost-reward matrix that includes costs associated with helping (e.g., effort, embarrassment, possible disgusting or distasteful experiences, possible physical harm, etc.), costs associated with not helping (mainly self-blame and perceived censure from others), rewards associated with helping (mainly praise from self, victim, and others), and rewards associated with not helping (mainly stemming from continuation of other activities). (Piliavin et al., 1969, p. 298)

On the basis of the proposed model, Piliavin and Piliavin (1972) made the following predictions:

(a) As arousal increases, the probability of the observer making *some* response to the emergency increases. (b) Holding arousal constant, as costs for *not* helping increase, the probability of helping as opposed to leaving the scene increases. (c) As costs *for* helping increase, the probability of direct intervention decreases and the probability of indirect help or leaving the scene decreases. (p. 353)

In order to confirm the predictions derived from the model, the Piliavins carried out two experiments. The first (Piliavin et al., 1969) was performed in a subway train in New York. Four teams consisting of a victim, a model, and two observers staged an accident in which the victim staggered forward and collapsed. The victim remained on the floor waiting for assistance. If no one intervened, the model helped the victim to his feet. Three of the victims were white and one was black. On some trials each victim carried a liquor bottle and appeared to be drunk, and on other trials he carried a cane. The model was instructed to help the victim first in four different conditions, which differed in the timing of the intervention. Data recorded by observers included number, race, sex of the bystanders, speed of the helping responses, race and number of helpers, movement out of the place where the victim collapsed, and spontaneous comments. The results of the experiment showed that in contrast to Latané and Darley's findings the bystanders were very helpful. Help was given on 100 percent of the trials when the victim appeared to be sober, and on 50 percent of the trials when the victim appeared to be drunk. Helping a drunk may involve much cost. The help was usually given so quickly that the model did not succeed in carrying out his assignment. In 60 percent of the trials more than one helper assisted the victim. In general, the findings clearly showed that the expected decrease in the speed of responding, as group size increases, did not occur.

The second field experiment (Piliavin & Piliavin, 1972) was also carried out in a subway train and also involved the collapse of a victim. However, for two conditions the degree of emergency was varied. In one condition the victim bit an eyedropper full of red food coloring to simulate bleeding from the mouth. In the second condition, the victim showed no sign of "bleeding."

This experiment replicated the findings of the first experiment and did not confirm Latané and Darley's hypothesis about the diffusion of responsibility. As in the first experiment, the calculated cost of helping was an important determinant of intervention. In the blood condition bystanders helped less often than in the no-blood condition, apparently because they feared and were revolted by blood.

Although the hypotheses derived from the model were confirmed, the Piliavin and Piliavin model of response to emergency situations does not include two important elements. The model neglects the phase of awareness and interpretation in emergency situations, assuming that a person can understand what is happening immediately. In addition, the model does not incorporate the possible variables that may influence the cost-reward calculation.

In the next section a new model of the decision-making process of helping in emergency situations is proposed. This model is similar to the one proposed in the previous chapter for nonemergency situations. However, a number of elements were added to account for the difference in the way people react to emergency and nonemergency situations.

A MODEL OF HELPING IN EMERGENCY

The proposed model analyzes the decision-making process of the bystander who has to decide whether or not to intervene in the emergency. Figure 2 represents the elements of the decision-making process and the variables that affect the decision. The major variance in behavior in emergency situations will be determined by the interpretation of the situation, attribution of responsibility about the victim, and various rewards and costs the bystanders calculate.

In the first phase of helping in an emergency a person becomes aware that something is happening. The awareness of an unusual and strange event causes physiological arousal without understanding what exactly is happening. A person may

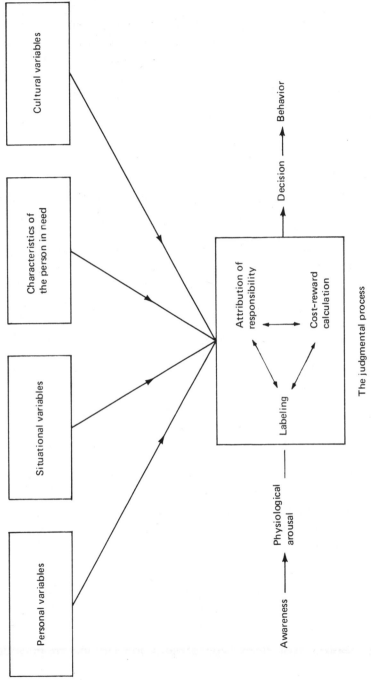

FIGURE 2 The decision-making model of helping in emergency.

see someone falling in a subway, hear someone crying, or notice a fist fight, but in the first second he is unable to label the situation; he only feels arousal. Many emergency situations are ambiguous. For example, fist fighting in the street may indicate an assault or merely a game among friends; smoke coming through a window may indicate fire or merely steam from boiling water.

The next phase in the decision-making process consists of three judgments. The person must label the situation as an emergency or nonemergency, understanding what is happening enough to decide why the victim is in trouble (to attribute responsibility), and calculate the cost-reward involved in helping and not helping. These three judgments interact with each other, that is, one judgment affects the other two. For example, if a person judges the victim who has collapsed in the street to be drunk, it would be costly to intervene, and therefore he will not label the situation an emergency. Similarly, if a person is in a big hurry, he may arbitrarily judge the victim to be drunk because it would be very costly for him to stop. The judgmental process is influenced by four types of variables: personal, situational, characteristics of the victim, and cultural. (These variables were defined in the previous chapter.) After making the three judgments, the person decides whether or not to intervene. Each phase of the decision-making process will be discussed separately.

Awareness

In the emergency situation a victim may make a direct or indirect appeal for help, or no appeal at all. A direct appeal consists of personally asking the bystander for help. For example, in a study by Suedfeld et al. (1972) a female approached the subject and said, "My friend [pointing to the male E] isn't feeling well. Would you help us?" (p. 19). In this study, 99 percent of the subjects agreed to help. An indirect appeal may consist of a cry from the victim (e.g., Latané & Rodin, 1969). In a third type of situation the victim may not emit any appeal for help; the victim may collapse or faint in a public place (e.g., Piliavin et al., 1969; Staub & Baer, 1974). In the last two situations, an indirect appeal or no appeal, the bystander is not involved immediately and after noticing that something has happened judges the nature of the situation. In the first situation, a direct appeal, the victim defines the situation for the bystander. In fact, he labels it and as a result increases the likelihood that the bystander will intervene.

Physiological Arousal

It is assumed that the observation of an emergency situation elicits a state of physiological arousal in the bystander. Unfortunately, none of the helping in emergency experiments has measured the emotional reactions of bystanders. The only direct evidence for this assumption comes from the study by Lazarus (1968) in which he showed the subjects films of an industrial accident and found that this stimulus situation caused emotional arousal. A number of other researchers reported emotional arousal in subjects who participated in experiments that investigated helping in an emergency. For example, Darley, Teger, and Lewis (1973) said, "Generally in all conditions, subjects individually showed similar degrees of initial startle response and facial expressions indicating concern or arousal" (p. 398). Bickman (1971) reported that "49% of the Ss spontaneously reported that they were frightened by the incident. They expressed that they were shaking, upset, or that their hearts were pounding" (p. 372). Similar observations were reported by Darley and Batson (1973), Schwartz and Clausen (1970), and Smith et al. (1972). However, further research is needed to validate this assumption.

Labeling

Labeling the situation is a simple judgment when the victim makes an appeal for help. By making an appeal, the victim labels the situation and the bystander realizes the nature of the emergency. Indeed a study by Yakimovich and Saltz (1971) found that when the victim called out for help, 81 percent of the subjects helped, but when the victim only groaned as though in pain, only 29 percent helped. Similarly in a study by

Bickman (1972) when another bystander defined a crash and a victim's scream as an emergency accident, the subjects reported the emergency very fast. However, when the same accident occurred and nobody labeled it as an emergency, the subjects did not rush to report it. Bickman summarized this finding by suggesting that "subjects' definition of the emergency and their helping behavior was influenced by the interpretation of the situation given by a confederate" (p. 444).

Most emergency situations are ambiguous. Therefore, the bystander must judge the situation and label it as an emergency before he may decide to help. In the Latané and Darley (1968) study, smoke might have represented fire, but it might have been nothing more than steam from a radiator. In the Latané and Rodin (1969) experiment, a crash and the sounds of sobbing might have indicated a woman with a badly injured leg, but it might have meant nothing more than a slight sprain and a good deal of chagrin.

The interpretation of the situation by aroused bystanders is determined by the cognitive elements of the situation (see Schachter, 1964). Individuals are looking for environmental cues to help them label the situation. In this vein, Schachter has postulated and demonstrated that in situations involving some degree of ambiguity, the perceived reactions of others may play an important role in determining how the situation is interpreted. Thus, the presence of others may be the critical variable that affects the decision process of intervention in an emergency situation.

Clark and Word (1972), who manipulated the ambiguity of the emergency situation, have shown that characteristics of the emergency situation are important determinants of whether an individual or a group is likely to respond to the pleas of an individual in distress. Subjects who volunteered to participate in a discussion about sexual issues witnessed an emergency under two conditions. A confederate posing as a maintenance employee entered an adjacent room carrying a ladder and a venetian blind. After three minutes, he pushed the ladder to the floor; in the low-ambiguity condition he did not emit any verbal pleas. The results of this study showed that subjects confronted with an ambiguous emergency situation, particularly when in the presence of others, helped less often than individuals who were exposed to a nonambiguous situation. Latané and Rodin (1969) explained this finding:

> In public, Americans generally wish to appear poised and in control of themselves. Thus, it is possible for a state of "pluralistic ignorance" to develop in which each bystander is led by the *apparent* lack of concern of the others to interpret the situation as being less serious than he would if he were alone. (p. 199)

Several experiments (e.g., Bickman, 1972; Darley et al., 1973; Latané & Darley, 1968; Ross & Braband, 1973; Smith et al., 1972) confirmed the findings that when an ambiguous event occurs, the interpretation of the situation by an individual bystander is considerably influenced by the way in which other bystanders react to the event.

Attribution of Responsibility

The bystander tries to infer the causes of an emergency by attributing specific intentions and dispositions to the victim on the basis of the observed behavior (Heider, 1958; Jones & Davis, 1965). The basic judgment involves attribution of the causes as being either beyond the victim's control (external causes) or within his control (internal causes). Bystanders are reluctant to help a person who needs help because of internal reasons, as evidenced in an experiment by Piliavin et al. (1969). In their study an "ill" victim (carrying a cane) who collapsed in a train received significantly more help faster than a "drunk" victim (smelling of liquor and carrying a liquor bottle). One of the reasons that the drunk victim was helped less was that he was "in part responsible for his own victimization" (p. 298).

Cost-Reward Calculation

The person facing an emergency situation calculates his costs and rewards for helping and not helping, with important consequences for the kind of decision he will make. It had been pointed out that often helping in an emergency can involve high costs.

The potential costs of helping may include personal danger. The intervening bystander may find himself confronted with such serious perils as a criminal or a fire. The act of helping always includes such costs as effort expended and time lost. In addition, the victim may reject the bystander's help, embarrass him, or even attack him.

Costs of helping can also be psychological. The helper may ridicule himself if he misinterprets the situation, he may have feelings of incompetence and failure if the help is ineffective, or other bystanders may disapprove his action. The costs of nonintervention are especially psychological. The bystander who doesn't help may feel shame, guilt, and empathic distress at a victim's suffering. The public may disapprove the nonintervener, and in some cases he may even face criminal prosecution. Obviously, differences in personal attributes such as perception of personal responsibility and ties to conventional norms are extremely important in the determination of self-blame and response to potential censure. Rewards for not helping consist of all those benefits associated with the activities that would be interrupted by helping. Potential rewards for helping are mostly psychological, such as feelings of competence, satisfaction, raised self-esteem, good mood, and praise and gratitude from the victim.

Latané and Darley (1970) said that the decision whether or not to help is very difficult, with a choice between two possibilities, both of them bad. The cost-reward calculation may certainly affect the labeling process or the attribution of responsibility, other elements of the judgmental process. As Latané and Darley suggested:

> The easiest way out of such a conflict is for the bystander to convince himself that no emergency really exists. If he can keep from noticing the emergency . . . if he can decide that the strange things he sees do not signify an emergency (as many subjects seemed to do in the smoke study), or if he can decide that the situation is not serious and that intervention would be inappropriate (as many subjects in the injured woman study decided), he need feel no conflict about whether or not to intervene. (pp. 80–81)

As was previously discussed, the experiments by Piliavin et al. (1969), and Piliavin and Piliavin (1972) demonstrated that the cost involved in intervention was a determinant of helping behavior. Calculation of costs-rewards, together with labeling and attribution of responsibility, are the judgments that determine the decision of the bystander whether or not to help. These judgments are affected by four types of variables, which will be discussed further.

Personal Variables

Personal variables consist of demographic characteristics and personality traits of the potential helper. Researchers have related a number of personal characteristics to helping in emergencies in a search for those variables that affect the decision whether or not to help.

Demographic Characteristics

Sex. Several studies have compared the intervention in emergency situations of males and females. Although Latané and Darley (1970) did not find any sex differences in their study of an epileptic seizure emergency, later experiments did find strong sex differences. For example, in a study by Piliavin and Piliavin (1972), 94 percent of the first helpers were males, although only 47 percent of the subjects were male. Similar results were obtained by Borofsky, Stollak, and Messé (1971), and Piliavin et al. (1969).

Schwartz and Clausen (1970) found that the presence of other bystanders affected the reaction of females but not of males. Females tended to help less and slower in the presence of others than when they were alone; 31 percent of females who thought they were alone intervened indirectly as compared to only 3 percent of females who believed others were present. However, on comparisons of direct intervention, the proportion of female helpers who intervened did not change with the addition of other bystanders. Male helpers were not affected by the presence of other bystanders in their direct and indirect intervention. Possibly females tend to help in emergencies less than males because the costs to females for helping in emergency situations might be higher than for males. Females are reluctant to intervene in situations where physical effort is involved, or where possible consequences are ambiguous.

Race. Studies by Piliavin and Piliavin (1972) and by Piliavin et al. (1969) found that the race of the victim made no difference to the helper when the cost involved was low. However, in the high-cost conditions the bystanders tended to help more the victims of their own race than those of other races. Piliavin et al. (1969) noted that "same-race helping, particularly of the drunk, can be explained by differential costs for not helping (less censure if one is of opposite race) and, with the drunk, differential costs for helping (more fear if of different race)" (p. 298).

Latané and Darley (1970) correlated eleven biographical variables with the speed with which the bystanders reported the epileptic seizure. Only two of these correlations reached the acceptable level of significance: the size of community in which the bystander grew up, and the occupation of the bystander's father. Subjects who lived in small communities and came from the lower middle class tended to be the most helpful.

Personality Traits

Several investigators have searched for a relationship between personality traits and helping behavior in emergencies. Staub (1974) assessed subjects' tendency to ascribe responsibility, social responsibility, machiavellianism, beliefs about human nature, level of moral development, values, and locus of control. He found that all these measures were significantly related to helping behavior.

Liebhart (1972) measured the person's sympathetic orientation and inclination to take instrumental action for the relief of his own hypothetical discomfort. Liebhart hypothesized that those individuals who experience emotional arousal accompanied by empathy when they observe an emergency, and have a tendency to take action in order to reduce that arousal, will tend to intervene. The data supported this prediction when subjects were high on both sympathetic orientation and instrumental activity. Liebhart suggested that sympathetic capability is an important factor in helping in emergency, and the extent to which sympathy will lead to the helping behavior depends on one's desire to get rid of an unpleasant emotional state caused by the observation of the emergency situation.

Schwartz and Clausen (1970) predicted that individuals who tend to ascribe responsibility for moral decisions to themselves, as measured by Ascription of Responsibility Scale, tend to intervene in emergency situations. The results indicated that the proportion of subjects who emerged from a room in response to an emergency was substantially larger among those who scored below the median on AR (Ascription of Responsibility Scale) than among those who scored above the median.

In contrast, several researchers did not find personality traits to be useful predictors of helping behavior in emergencies. Darley and Batson (1973) measured different conceptions of religiosity; Darley and Latané (1968) measured machiavellianism, anomie, authoritarianism, need for approval, and social responsibility; Korte (1971) measured difference, autonomy, and submissiveness; Yakimovich and Saltz (1971) measured New Leftism, trustworthiness, independence, altruism, locus of control, and general activity. In all these studies none of these measures came close to being significantly related to helping behavior. All these researchers suggested that situational variables appear to be more crucial than personality variables in determining helping in emergency behavior.

Situational Variables

The presence of other bystanders has been considered as the most potent variable that determines whether or not a person will intervene in an emergency (Latané & Darley, 1970). Most of the laboratory studies (e.g., Bickman, 1971, 1972; Darley & Latané, 1968; Latané & Rodin, 1969; Smith et al., 1972) have confirmed the finding that an individual who witnesses a potential emergency alone is more likely to intervene than one who witnesses it with other bystanders. These investigators have hypothesized that the presence of others plays a dual role: the others supply cues as to appropriate behavior in the face of novel stimuli, and at the same time they allow a diffusion of responsibility, such that no one person can be blamed for not having intervened.

In order to investigate the effect of the others' presence, experimenters manipulated a variety of combinations and situations. Darley and Latané (1968) and Latané and Rodin (1969) tested the reactions of pairs of friends faced with an emergency. They found that although pairs of friends were inhibited from helping when compared to the condition where a person was alone, they intervened significantly faster than pairs of strangers. People may be less likely to fear embarrassment in front of friends than before strangers, and friends are less likely to misinterpret each others' inaction than are strangers.

In another experiment by Smith et al. (1972), male subjects observed a victim under one of three conditions: alone, in the presence of a confederate supposedly similar to themselves in attitudes, or in the presence of a dissimilar confederate; the confederate in both cases did not respond to the emergency. They found that the greatest inhibition of helping behavior occurred in the presence of a similar confederate because the subject avoided helping to show compatibility with the confederate's behavior.

In a later experiment of Smith, Vanderbilt, and Callen (1973), male subjects were exposed to an emergency situation with a confederate who was either nonreactive or alarmed by the emergency, and who was either similar or dissimilar to the subject. While 60 percent of the subjects intervened when the confederate was alarmed by the emergency, only 13 percent did so when the confederate was nonreactive. In addition, when the alarmed confederate was similar, subjects tended to intervene faster than when the alarmed confederate was dissimilar. These results indicate that the other bystander, by helping label the situation, exerts influence on the subject's helping behavior.

In this vein, Darley et al. (1973) suggested that the spatial position of bystanders may be an important determinant of communication among them and thus affect helping in an emergency. When subjects were seated face-to-face, 80 percent responded to a simulated crash, as compared to 20 percent of the subjects who were not facing each other. It is possible that the face-to-face situation facilitated communication among the bystanders, who could observe each other's emotional reactions.

Ross (1971) and Ross and Braband (1973) investigated the

diffusion of responsibility among subjects in two situations. In the first study (Ross, 1971), college students encountered an emergency either with two nonreacting student confederates or with two nonreacting child confederates. They found that the subjects responded more rapidly when they were with children than when they were with other adults. The presence of children did not diffuse the responsibility to intervene. In the second study (Ross & Braband, 1973), subjects encountered an emergency either alone or paired with a blind confederate or with a normally sighted confederate. Subjects paired with the blind person responded to the emergency (odorless smoke propelled into the room) that threatened them as frequently and as rapidly as subjects who were alone. But when the emergency threatened another person in another room, injured and groaning in pain, subjects paired with a blind confederate, responded as infrequently and as slowly as subjects paired with a sighted confederate. This study indicated that the other bystander's characteristic (e.g., blindness) may be a determinant if he can provide a cue for the appropriate response and diffuse the responsibility. In the situation of odorless smoke, since the blind bystander could not react to the emergency, the subject apparently felt responsibility for him. In the other emergency the blind person could intervene as well, and therefore the subjects diffused their responsibility.

Darley and Latané (1968) found that the introduction of a medically competent male bystander had no important effect on the speed of reaction of female subjects. But Schwartz and Clausen (1970) found a substantial reduction in rates and speed of helping associated with this manipulation. Schwartz and Clausen explained the difference between their finding and Darley and Latané's by the difference of competence manipulation employed by the two studies. Darley and Latané's competence bystander transmitted normative expectations of behavior, which encouraged the subjects to intervene, but Schwartz and Clausen's competence bystander merely described his capabilities. Therefore, the subjects reduced their feelings of responsibility and did not rush to help.

Darley and Batson (1973) hypothesized that people who are busy or rushing somewhere are less likely to spend time helping another person because any delay is costly for them. All their subjects reported to one building for the first part of the study and then were asked to report to another building for the second part, which consisted of giving a short talk either about the parable of the Good Samaritan (topic relevant to helping) or about a topic not relevant to helping. As each subject left the first building, time pressure was manipulated so as to make him think he was either early, on time, or late for the scheduled talk. On his way to the second building, he saw the victim slumped in a doorway with his head down, eyes close, not moving. As the subject went by, the victim coughed twice and groaned, but kept his head down. The results showed that 63 percent of the early students helped, 45 percent of the on-time students helped, and only 10 percent of the late students helped. The nature of the talk did not have any effect on the helping behavior.

Another situational variable, the position of the victim in relation to the bystanders, was investigated by Staub and Baer (1974), who hypothesized that more helping will be given to a victim when escape from the victim's distress is difficult. In their study the victim collapsed on the sidewalk either in front of the subject or on the other side of the street. The results showed that although all the subjects noticed the emergency, those who encountered the victim on their way helped more than those who saw the victim on the other side of the street. It is possible that the latter subjects felt that it is not costly not to intervene because they could pretend that they did not know the victim and therefore these subjects minimized their involvement.

Characteristics of the Victim

Few studies have investigated the effect of the victim's characteristics on bystanders' helping behavior. Borofsky et al. (1971) simulated a situation in which either one male was beating another male, one female was beating another female, one male was beating a female, or one female was beating a male. The results showed surprisingly that males did not interfere more when the "victim" in the fight was a female; in fact they tended to interfere less. The authors suggested that males failed to interfere because they were deriving some kind of vicarious sexual and/or hostile gratification from seeing an injured woman.

Another investigated variable was similarity between the potential helper and the victim. A study by Suedfeld et al. (1972) was carried out during the April 1971 peace demonstration in Washington, D.C. A young woman approached different demonstrators, who were opposed to President Nixon's Vietnam policy, and asked them to help her male friend, who was ill. This male was displaying either a "Support Nixon" or a "Dump Nixon" sign. The experimenters hypothesized that because of similarity of the victim to themselves, the demonstrators would be more likely to help the victim carrying a "Dump Nixon" sign than the one carrying a "Support Nixon" sign. The results confirmed the hypothesis: the victim displaying the "Dump Nixon" sign received more help than the victim displaying the "Support Nixon" sign.

Cultural Variables

Milgram (1970) has stated that nonhelping is more common in cities than in small towns, and has attributed this to differences in social style of life. People who live in big cities are "stimulus overloaded" and live in "social anonymity." Further, in large cities people may generally be inhibited from helping because of fear of physical vulnerability—a concern supported by urban crime statistics. On the other hand in a small town people tend to know each other and feel more social responsibility toward each other. The only study that refers to subcultural differences was carried out by Clark and Word (1972). In contrast to other studies, which were carried out in the northern parts of the United States (e.g., Latané & Rodin, 1969), Clark and Word's study was carried out in the South. In this experiment all the subjects intervened and the number of other bystanders did not have any effect on helping behavior. The researchers attributed the findings partially to population differences, suggesting that a reaction in a southern environment may be different than in a larger northern urban area.

SUMMARY

The proposed model of decision making in emergency situations postulates that bystanders who are emotionally aroused react on the basis of cognitive-mediated judgments. The judgment process consists of three elements: labeling the situation, attributing responsibility for the victim's situation, and calculating the cost-reward matrix for intervention. The cognitive process of the judgment can be described as three different judgments, which are interrelated. It is impossible to isolate one of these elements because one judgment is affected by another. The cognitive process is influenced by different variables.

Most of the studies focused on one situational variable, namely, the presence of other bystanders in the emergency situation. Most investigators have explained the failure of bystanders to intervene in emergencies by referring to the variables related among bystanders, i.e., group size, presence of others, relationship among bystanders, etc. At the same time many different variables were completely ignored. Future research will have to determine what are the major cues and characteristics of different emergency situations.

This type of research must be done in naturalistic settings, free of any experimenter effects, subject effects, or "demand characteristics" of the manipulated situation. At the same time other important variables should be incorporated into the research: personal variables, characteristics of the victim, and cultural variables.

In a recent paper McGuire (1973) suggested a new paradigm for research in social psychology. Some of his suggestions could be utilized in studying helping behavior in emergency situations. He suggested that social psychologists should take into account multiple and bidirectional causality among social variables. He also proposed that psychologists should focus on the more observational method. The emergency situation can be staged or in some cases actually observed (e.g., floods, tornadoes, etc.). Another way to study helping behavior in an emergency would be to collect data about events that have occurred in the past. For example, it is possible to interview bystanders who have witnessed an emergency. All these methods should help us better understand the dynamics of helping in an emergency.

6

RECIPROCITY BEHAVIOR

A reciprocity act is one type of prosocial behavior. It occurs when a person who has received help or a favor reciprocates by helping or returning a favor to the original donor. However, reciprocity behavior is considered to be prosocial only if it is done voluntarily for the sake of restitution and without anticipation of external rewards. That means that a recipient of help must decide to reciprocate without external pressures. Reciprocity initiated as a result of a threat or anticipation of external rewards is not considered a prosocial act. However, a recipient may feel an internal urge to reciprocate previously received help or favors. In fact, a number of theories attempted to explain the basis of reciprocity behavior by assuming that a person feels an obligation to reciprocate.

THEORETICAL BASIS OF RECIPROCITY BEHAVIOR

The theories that attempt to explain the basis of reciprocity behavior derive from the exchange approach. The basic proposition of the exchange approach states that "Persons that give much to others try to get much from them, and persons that get much from others are under pressure to give much to them" (Homans, 1958, p. 606). Thus, the exchange approach postulates that individuals who receive favors or help are expected to reciprocate. Each of the specific theories will be reviewed separately.

Distributive Justice Theory

Homans (1961), a proponent of the exchange approach, suggested the existence of a "distributive justice" principle. According to this principle, individuals who are in exchange relations compare their profits from the exchange by subtracting costs (e.g., loss of time, effort, money) from rewards (e.g., satisfaction, pride, money) in relation to their investments.

> A man in an exchange relation with another will expect that the rewards of each man be proportional to his costs—the greater the rewards, the greater the costs—and that the net rewards, or profits, of each man be proportional to his investments—the greater the investments, the greater the profit. (p. 75)

The investments are the relevant characteristics of the individuals in interaction that are brought into the exchange. They include such characteristics as education, age, motivation, or knowledge. When the compared proportionality between profits and investments does not accrue from social exchange, the rule of distributive justice is violated.

The donor who helps and the recipient who receives the help are considered to be in an exchange relation. In this exchange, a donor incurs some costs and the recipient receives some rewards. The comparison of profits between the donor and the recipient indicates that the distributive justice failed. Schematically, the comparison appears as follows:

$$\frac{\text{Recipient's rewards} - \text{costs (profits)}}{\text{Recipient's investments}} > \frac{\text{donor's rewards} - \text{costs (profits)}}{\text{donor's investments}}$$

According to Homans, the recipient, who has a more favorable ratio of profits to investments than the donor, feels an obligation to repay the donor. Such an obligation derives from feelings of guilt, which are proportional to the extent of the advantage.

Equity Theory

Equity theory, proposed by Adams (1965), is similar to the notion of distributive justice. Adams postulated that in human interactions individuals exchange inputs for outcomes. Inputs are contributions that a person brings into an exchange. They consist of skill, seniority effort, knowledge, etc. Inputs correspond to Homans' concepts of investments and costs. Outcomes are the receipts that a person gets in an exchange. Outcome can have positive value (e.g., money, satisfaction, or prestige) and negative value (e.g., dissatisfaction, boredom, or sickness). Outcomes correspond to Homans' concepts of rewards and costs. Furthermore, individuals in exchange interactions tend to compare the ratio of their outputs to inputs with other people who are *relevant* to that particular exchange. Adams suggested that "inequity exists for Person whenever he perceives that the ratio of his outcomes to inputs and the ratio of Other's outcomes to Other's inputs are unequal" (p. 280).

In the interaction in which the recipient was helped by the donor there appears to be inequity. The ratio of the recipient's outcomes to inputs exceeds the ratio of the donor. This inequity can be represented schematically as follows:

$$\frac{\text{Recipient's outcomes}}{\text{Recipient's inputs}} > \frac{\text{donor's outcomes}}{\text{donor's inputs}}$$

The theory further assumes that inequity results in adversive feelings.

> First, the presence of inequity in Person creates tension in him. The tension is proportional to the magnitude of inequity present. Second, the tension created in Person will motivate him to eliminate or reduce it. (Adams, 1965, p. 283)

A recipient who experiences inequity can reduce it in a number of ways. He can change the outcomes of the donor by reciprocating the previously received help. He can leave the field by discontinuing further interaction with the donor. He can also distort cognitively either his inputs and/or outcomes or the donor's inputs and/or outcomes. The recipient for example may decide that the donor enjoyed giving the help that increased the donor's outcomes, or the recipient may decide that receiving help was very costly, thus decreasing self-outcomes.

Reciprocity Theory

Another theory that derives from the exchange approach is reciprocity theory. Reciprocity theory formulated by Gouldner (1960) postulates the presence of a universal norm of reciprocity which states: "(1) People should help those who have helped them, and (2) people should not injure those who have helped them" (p. 171). According to Gouldner's reasoning, reciprocity implies the internalization of a norm that obliges a recipient to repay his benefactor. The strength of this obligation varies according to the needs of both parties engaged in the exchange, the resources of the donor, as well as the motives of the donor and the constraints of the giving act. Gouldner further states that the norm of reciprocity has an important role in stabilizing human relations in society. It

> engenders motives for returning benefits even when power differences might invite exploitation. The norm thus safeguards powerful people against the temptation of their own status; it motivates and regulates reciprocity as an exchange pattern, serving to inhibit the emergence of exploitative relations. (p. 174)

In addition, the norm serves as a starting mechanism for human interactions. A person who initiates an exchange by helping another person is confident that the recipient will reciprocate. Society enforces the existence of the norm by applying negative sanctions to those recipients who do not repay their debts.

The norm of reciprocity is less general than the equity norm. Leventhal, Weiss, and Long (1969) pointed out that the equity norm arises whenever outcomes are disproportional to inputs, irrespective of the reasons for the disproportionality. In contrast, the norm of reciprocity is greatly influenced by the perceived cause of the disparity between inputs and outcomes. A person will be motivated to reciprocate, not merely to reduce inequity, only when he believes that the other is directly responsible for his benefiting from an act.

Indebtedness Theory

In an attempt to analyze the process underlying reciprocity, Greenberg (1968; in press) has reformulated the concept of the norm of reciprocity in terms of a psychological state of indebtedness (i.e., a state wherein a person feels an obligation to repay a benefit). According to Greenberg (in press), indebtedness is an unpleasant arousal state characterized by alertness to cues relevant to the reduction of an obligation. This state "may be viewed as a special case of cognitive dissonance" (Greenberg, 1968, p. 4), in that one is aware of a need to reciprocate (because of normative requirements), but one has not yet reciprocated. Indebtedness thus has motivational properties such that the greater its magnitude the greater the efforts to reduce it. The magnitude of indebtedness is assumed to be a function of four factors:

1. The quantity and quality of the recipients rewards and costs in comparison to the donor's rewards and costs. The more rewards the recipient received and the more costs the donor incurred, the greater the indebtedness the recipient experiences. (Although a person may feel indebtedness just because of a donor's incurred costs for an unsuccessful attempt to help, in general individuals feel more indebtedness as a result of net rewards.)
2. A recipient feels the most indebtedness when the perceived locus of causality of the donor's help resides within him. A recipient feels less indebtedness if the donor initiated the help himself and the least indebtedness when the locus of causality resides in the environment.
3. The magnitude of indebtedness depends also on the recipient's perception of the donor's motive in giving the help. The greatest indebtedness will be experienced by the recipient if the donor gave an intentional and personal help.

4. Finally, the magnitude of indebtedness depends on the cues received by others. Others may indicate verbally or nonverbally what the recipient ought to do. The indication that the recipient ought to reciprocate increases the feeling of indebtedness.

Individuals who experience indebtedness attempt to reduce it. The reduction of indebtedness can be accomplished either through reciprocity behavior or by cognitively restructuring the situation. Cognitive restructure of the situation can be done by reevaluating the quantity and quality of the resources received and given up by the recipient and the donor, by reassessing the locus of causality of the donor's help, by reassessing the donor's motives for helping, or by reassessing the opinions of others in the situation. Greenberg suggested that the recipient will prefer cognitive restructuring as a way to reduce indebtedness to the extent that

(a) cognitions associated with the helping act are ambiguous, (b) there are few witnesses to the helping act, (c) further interaction with the donor and witnesses is not anticipated, and (d) the recipient perceives little or no opportunity to reciprocate. (Greenberg, in press)

Empirical support for the conceptualization of an aversive state of indebtedness was found in a number of studies. A study by Greenberg and Shapiro (1971) found that a person was more willing to ask for needed help, and thus become indebted, when he anticipated being able to return the favor than when he did not. In this study, the subjects were led to believe that the purpose of the experiment was to investigate a performance of physically disabled workers. Each subject was assigned to play a role of a person with a serious motor handicap (arm placed in sling) and the confederate was assigned to play the role of a person with a serious visual handicap (patch over eye and sunglasses). The task consisted of constructing paper boxes from sheets of paper with scissors and a roll of Scotch tape. During the practice session the subject was given the impression that in order to meet the required quota of boxes he would need help from the confederate. After the practice session the subjects in the "anticipated reciprocity" condition were given the impression that the confederate would need help on the second task, which required proofreading of a passage. In the "no anticipated reciprocity" condition the subjects were given the impression that the confederate would be able to achieve the quota without help. Then the subject started to construct boxes. The dependent variable consisted of the subjects' asking or not asking for help. The results of the study showed that more subjects in the "no anticipated reciprocity" condition avoided seeking help than the subjects in the "anticipated reciprocity" condition. Greenberg and Shapiro explained these results by suggesting that "the aversiveness of indebtedness derives from the observation that the state of indebtedness constitutes a threat" (p. 290) to the person's status, power, and freedom of action. Additional reasons offered by Greenberg and Shapiro to explain the aversiveness of indebtedness are that the state of indebtedness violates the recipient's sense of "ought" to reciprocate (Heider, 1958) and causes feelings of guilt.

Another postulate of indebtedness that has been investigated is the recipient's motivation to reduce the magnitude of indebtedness. Bar-Tal and Greenberg (1973) demonstrated that the more help one receives, the greater the tendency to examine and acquire information that would be useful in reciprocating. This study consisted of two experiments. In both experiments the subjects as a first task were instructed to assemble a jigsaw puzzle. During the task some subjects received varying amounts of help from the confederate and some did not receive any help. Prior to working on the second puzzle, the subjects were permitted to examine a booklet containing solutions to their own and the confederate's second puzzle. In addition, the subjects were informed that on the second task they would be able to interact and exchange information. The results from the first experiment showed that the recipients of help spent more time studying the solutions of the confederate's puzzle than subjects who did not receive help. In the second experiment, the study time was held constant and the dependent variable consisted of amount of information correctly learned concerning the solution to the confederate's puzzle. In line with the results of the first experiment, the subjects who received prior help acquired more information concerning the confederate's puzzle than those who did not receive prior help. The results of these two experiments supported the hypothesis that individuals are actively looking for opportunities to repay the other and thereby reduce the state of indebtedness.

Other Explanations of Reciprocity Behavior

The reviewed theories of distributive justice, equity, reciprocity, and indebtedness agree that individuals who receive help or favors feel an obligation to reciprocate. However, it should be pointed out that a number of other explanations were also offered to account for the empirical evidence of reciprocity behavior. One possibility is that individuals reciprocate simply because of the prescription of an altruistic norm (Norm of Social Responsibility), which states that individuals should help those who are dependent upon them (Berkowitz & Daniels, 1963). According to this explanation, the help received from the donor heightens the salience of the norm, thereby inducing the recipient to help in return. Goranson and Berkowitz (1966), who compared the potency of the norms of reciprocity and social responsibility, concluded that "the responsibility norm is somewhat weaker than the norm prescribing reciprocity" (p. 231).

A second possible explanation derives from a consideration of attraction between the recipient and donor. According to this explanation, the recipient helps the donor because he is attracted to him. However, studies by Greenberg, Block, and Silverman (1971), Nemeth (1970b), and Stapleton, Nacci, and Tedeschi (1973) found no relationship between attraction and reciprocity.

A third explanation, which is somewhat similar to the attraction explanation, states that recipients who received help feel "a warm glow of success" (Isen, 1970; Isen & Levin, 1972), that is, they are in a good mood and consequently they act charitably. Support for this interpretation is found in the work of Isen and Levin (1972), who demonstrated that people put in a good mood by being given cookies were more helpful than control subjects. Research by Bar-Tal and Greenberg (1974), Greenglass (1969), and Regan (1971) demonstrated that the "warm glow of success" by itself cannot explain the act of reciprocity. Finally, Greenberg (in press) suggested, following the exchange theorists (Blau, 1964; Homans, 1961), that "reciprocity may be motivated by the recipient's desire to receive future rewards from the donor" (p. 20). Although this explanation was not directly challenged by empirical research, in most of the studies the subjects are strangers and they probably do not expect to see each other in the future.

A MODEL OF RECIPROCITY BEHAVIOR

Numerous studies (e.g., Bar-Tal & Greenberg, 1974; Berkowitz & Daniels, 1964; Goranson & Berkowitz, 1966; Greenberg & Frisch, 1972; Greenglass, 1969; Muir & Weinstein, 1962; Nemeth, 1970b; Pruitt, 1968; Schopler & Thompson, 1968; Wilke & Lanzetta, 1970) have demonstrated the tendency of individuals to reciprocate favors. The basic assumption underlying these studies is that individuals who receive help or favors feel an obligation to repay their debts.

Although these studies support the existence of an obligation to reciprocate, Gouldner (1960) has indicated that the norm of reciprocity is contingent upon the number of variables:

> The value of the benefit and hence the debt is in proportion to and varies with—among other things—the intensity of the recipient's need at the time the benefit was bestowed ("a friend in need . . ."), the resources of the donor ("he gave although he could ill afford it"), the motives imputed to the donor ("without thought of gain"), and the nature of the constraints which are perceived to exist or to be absent ("he gave of his own free will . . ."). Thus the obligations imposed by the norm of reciprocity may vary with the *status* of the participants within a society. (p. 171)

Following Gouldner, many recent studies have concentrated on the search for variables that affect the willingness of the recipient to reciprocate.

In this part of the chapter, a model of the decision-making process of reciprocity behavior is proposed. This model analyzes the decision-making process of the recipient taking into account possible variables that may affect the decision whether or not to reciprocate. Figure 3 represents schematically the elements of

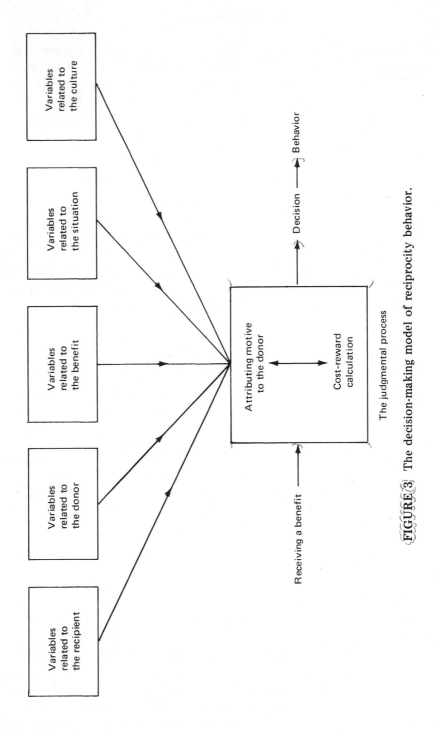

FIGURE 3 The decision-making model of reciprocity behavior.

the decision-making process and the variables that affect that decision.

In the first phase, a person receives a benefit from a donor. In the next phase, the recipient makes attributions about the donor's motives and calculates the rewards and costs involving reciprocity behavior. These two judgments are interrelated. For example, the recipient may decide that the donor had an ulterior motive while helping him and therefore it will not be costly to refuse reciprocity, or it can be costly to reciprocate and therefore the recipient may decide that the donor had ulterior motives. The judgmental process is influenced by five types of variables: variables related to the recipient, variables related to the donor, variables related to the benefit, variables related to the situation, and variables related to the culture. After the judgmental process, the recipient decides whether to recipro-cate or not. If the recipient decided positively, the behavior can be carried out only to the extent that the recipient has the opportunity to reciprocate. Each phase of the decision-making process will be discussed separately.

Receiving a Benefit

A person may receive a benefit in a number of ways. The benefit may be offered by the donor, or it may be imposed by the donor. How the recipient received the benefit is an important determinant in the recipient's attribution of the donor's motive. Ultimately, it determines the recipient's decision whether to reciprocate or not.

A study by Saxe and Greenberg (1974) manipulated the locus of help initiation. The recipient received either requested, offered, or imposed help. The subjects in this study were asked to imagine that they had to write a paper for a history course and then the three situations were outlined:

1. In the Requested help condition they are told: "While doing research for the paper you discover that a key book written on the topic has been checked out of the library by a fellow student. You phone the student and ask to borrow the book. He agrees and brings it over to your house Friday evening."
2. In the Offered help condition they are told: "Another student in the class informs you about a key book which has been written on

the topic and that he has checked it out of the library. He offers to lend you the book and brings it over to your house Friday evening."

3. In the Imposed help condition they are told: "Another student in the class informs you about a key book which has been written on the topic and that he has checked out of the library. He offers to lend you the book. You tell him that you really don't need the book, but he brings it over to your house Friday evening anyway." (p. 5)

The results of this study showed that the subjects felt the strongest obligation to reciprocate when they received requested help. Similar results were obtained by Muir and Weinstein (1962), who interviewed a large number of housewives. They found that the recipients feel more obligated to reciprocate if they have asked for a favor than if they are offered it. Schopler (1970) explained these findings by suggesting that the donor who offers or imposes help is likely to be seen as acting inappropriately and by ulterior motives. In such cases, the recipient does not tend to reciprocate as much as in the case in which he himself has requested help.

Attributing Motive to the Donor

Attributing motive to the donor is an important judgment that affects willingness to reciprocate. The recipient judges why the donor has helped him. If he decides that the donor provided help as a gracious act without any expectations of reward, then the recipient will attempt to reciprocate the received help. However, if the recipient decides that the donor has some ulterior motives in helping him, such as a donor's desire to obtain some future rewards, then the recipient will feel little obligation to reciprocate. A study by Tesser, Gatewood, and Driver (1968) directly investigated the effect of the donor's motives on feelings of gratitude. The subjects received three stories describing acts of help. For example, in one of the stories the aunt gave a picture either only to benefit the recipient, partially to benefit the recipient and partially to enhance her reputation, or solely to enhance her reputation. The subjects in this study expressed the most gratitude when the help was provided solely to benefit the recipient.

Cost-Reward Calculation

The recipient's behavior is affected by the calculated costs and rewards (Greenberg, Block, & Silverman, 1971). The act of reciprocity may involve such costs as effort expenditure, time lost, or even material help. Costs for not reciprocating are mostly psychological. The recipient may feel inequity, indebtedness, or guilt. He may also receive negative sanction such as disapproval from his group for violating the norm of reciprocity. The rewards for reciprocity are also mostly psychological. The recipient reduces his feelings of inequity and indebtedness on the one hand and on the other hand may feel competent and satisfied. Rewards for not reciprocating consist of all the activities that were not interrupted if the recipient reciprocated.

Variables Related to the Recipient

These variables consist of the recipient's stable disposition and demographic characteristics. Although few of the studies have investigated the effect of these variables on reciprocity behavior, it is possible to suggest that the recipient's personality traits and demographic characteristics do affect his decision whether or not to reciprocate. Thus, for example, Bar-Tal, Harmon, and Greenberg (1975) found that males are more reciprocity oriented than females and that females are altruistically oriented. In another study, by Thompson, Stroebe, and Schopler (1971), subjects were presented a questionnaire that described help given to either a powerful recipient (professor of the donor) or an unpowerful recipient (janitor). The results of this study showed that help given to a powerful recipient is more likely to be seen as selfishly motivated, and therefore was negatively evaluated more than help given to a less powerful recipient. However, this finding needs to be confirmed by experimental data.

Variables Related to the Donor

Variables related to the donor include the behaviors and characteristics of the donor as perceived by the recipient.

Empirical studies investigated a number of variables related to the donor.

Donor's Present Resources

A recipient is more willing to reciprocate if the donor has small resources than if he has large resources. It is costly in terms of indebtedness or inequity not to reciprocate a donor who provided help in spite of having small resources. Thus, for example, in a study by Tesser et al. (1968) the subjects expressed the most gratitude when they were asked to put themselves in a situation in which the aunt had given them a picture in spite of being in a poor economic situation. In the situation in which the aunt who gave the picture had a good economic situation, the subjects felt the least gratitude. These results were confirmed by Gergen, Ellsworth, Maslach and Seipel (1975) and Pruitt (1968).

Donor's Future Resources

Gouldner (1960) suggested that a reward is often provided to another person in order to build up credit in the hope that the other will reciprocate at a later date. Pruitt (1968) deduced from this postulate that the recipient will try to reciprocate especially to a donor with future resources in order "to build credit" for future exchanges. In this case, it will be potentially rewarding to reciprocate the received help. In his study, Pruitt (1968) found that the magnitude of resources the donor was expected to have in the future had a significant effect on reciprocity behavior. The subjects reciprocated more benefits received from a donor who was expected to have large future resources than from a donor expected to have small future resources.

Donor's Status

Thibaut and Riecken (1955) have demonstrated that the status of the donor is a variable that affects the recipient's perception of the donor's motive. It is thus assumed that status also affects the willingness of the recipient to reciprocate. In their study, the subjects asked for help from a high- and a low-status confederate, at the same time. Both confederates complied with the request. The subjects credited the high-status person with motives of friendliness and internally initiated help, while the low-status person was regarded as complying because of the recipient's external coercive power.

Donor's Relationship to Recipient

An experiment by Nadler, Fisher, and Streufert (1974) simulated a game of international negotiations in which a team representing national decision makers received an offer of aid from either an ally or an enemy donor. The authors found a pattern of results

> indicating that a higher percentage of ulterior motivation was attributed to enemy than to ally donors, that the likelihood of the donor using his donation for self-gain was perceived as greater for enemy than for ally donors, and ... that donations were perceived to reflect more donor effort and to be of greater value to the recipient when the donor was an ally than when the donor was an enemy. Taken as a whole, these observations indicate that an important moderator of the recipient's differential perceptions concerning the motivation associated with aid and the value of a donation is the quality of the relationship between the recipient and the donor at the time aid is given. (p. 283)

Another experiment by Bar-Tal et al. (1975) manipulated the relationship between the donor and the recipient by telling the subject that the donor was either a parent, a sibling, a friend, an acquaintance, or a stranger. The weaker the relationship, the more obligation was expressed by the subjects to reciprocate the received help. The subjects expressed the least obligation toward their parent. The help from the parent or sibling was perceived as required by the role, whereas help from a stranger was perceived as a gracious act.

Costs Incurred by Donor in Providing Benefit

Although a number of studies (e.g., Greenberg et al., 1971; Saxe & Greenberg, 1974) have investigated the effect of the costs incurred by the donor as a result of the act of help on the recipient's willingness to reciprocate, the results of these studies are confounded with other variables. The evidence from these studies indicates that an individual feels an obligation to reciprocate even in situations in which the donor unsuccessfully attempts to provide help while incurring costs. However, the studies consistently obtained results showing that the willingness to reciprocate is more a function of rewards received than costs incurred by the donor.

Past Help by Donor

The recipient's repayment is positively related to the level of help previously received from the donor. In order to continue an exchange relationship the recipient tries especially to reciprocate help from a donor who helped in the past. The results of an experiment by Pruitt (1968) provide evidence for such a hypothesis. For this experiment the subjects reciprocated more when the donor had, in the past, provided them with much help than when he had provided little help.

Donor's Act of Helping

The recipient also makes attribution about a donor's motives on the basis of the donor's act of helping. The donor may provide the benefit voluntarily, accidentally, or involuntarily. Nemeth (1970b) compared the reaction of the recipient to the voluntary versus compulsory help given by the donor. The subjects in this study were told that the objectives of the experiment were to investigate work performance and interview techniques in industrial settings. The subjects were instructed to proofread two typewritten sheets of paper and the confederate was assigned to work on a series of arithmetic and work problems. The manipulations were introduced by telling the subjects in the voluntary help condition that "you may, if you wish, help the other person with his task. Of course, you are under no obligation to do one thing or the other" (p. 305). In the compulsory help condition, the subjects were told, "Please help the other person with his task. It is important that we have enough time to finish the experiment" (p. 305). The confederate helped the subjects in both conditions. At the end of the experiment, the confederate asked the subject if he would be willing to help him by completing a survey and taking some additional surveys for completion by adults. The results of this study showed that the subjects took fewer surveys from the confederate who complied with instructions than from one who helped voluntarily. The subjects in the compulsory help condition perceived the donor's act as being carried out as a result of an external pressure and therefore were less willing to reciprocate that donor than a donor who himself initiated the help. Similarly, Greenberg and Frisch (1972) found that the recipient reciprocated more when the help was given to them deliberately than when it was given accidentally. The authors pointed out that the deliberate help told the recipient more about the donor's motivational dispositions than the accidental help. The deliberate help showed the recipient that the donor was internally motivated to help.

Variables Related to the Benefit

The quality and quantity of the reward provided by the donor are among the most important determinants of reciprocity behavior (Bar-Tal & Greenberg, 1973; Greenberg et al., 1971; Pruitt, 1968; Wilke & Lanzetta, 1970). The amount of reciprocated help has been viewed as a function of the amount of help received by the recipient. This linear relationship between the amount of help received and the amount of reciprocation was clearly demonstrated in the study by Wilke and Lanzetta (1970). In this study two subjects were instructed to play the roles of heads of two shipping departments in one company. Their task was to solve a problem that required each of them to ship goods in trucks and railroad cars. Each subject received the same sequence of 40 orders, and while they were assigned to separate rooms and led to believe that they would interact with each other, in reality they were receiving preprogrammed messages from the experimenter. The subjects were told that they could interact with each other by loaning carriers when one did not have sufficient transport resources. During the trials, the subjects had sufficient resources to handle the first 10 and the last 20 orders. On the second set of 10 trials, the subjects needed help and were provided with the loan either on 0, 2, 4, 6, 8, or 10 of the trials. During the last 20 trials, the subjects had the opportunity to reciprocate on 10 trials. The correlation between the help received and the help reciprocated was .71. Reciprocity was found to be proportional to the amount of prior help received from the donor. The more rewarded the recipients are the more they are willing to reciprocate.

Variables Related to the Situation

The situation as perceived by the recipient is another type of variable that affects the recipient's act of reciprocity. The perception of the situation may influence the recipient's attribution about the donor's motives and the recipient's cost and reward for reciprocating. A number of studies investigated the variables related to the situation. For a study by Brehm and Cole (1966) subjects were paired with the confederate and were told that the purpose of the experiment was to study projective testing techniques. At this point in the experiment the confederate asked for permission to leave for a few minutes. While the confederate had gone, the experimenter in a conversational tone asked the subject to participate in an impression formation study for another person. In the low importance condition, the experimenter told the subject that she was collecting data on impressions for an undergraduate student in sociology and that the subject "need not be too concerned with being careful or accurate on the rating scale since it was merely a class project on which the sociology student was practicing" (p. 422). In the high importance condition, the subject was told that the impression data was being collected for a professor who had received a large grant and that the test was very important so that the subject should be as careful and accurate as possible. When the experimenter left the room, the confederate returned and to half of the subjects he brought a soft drink for which he refused money. A few seconds later, the experimenter returned, and explained again the conditions of the impression formation experiment. When the subject and the confederate finished rating each other, the experimenter gave the confederate a stack of typing paper and asked to have them stacked into piles.

The results of the study showed that while 14 of the 15 subjects in the low importance condition reciprocated the favor, in the high importance condition only 2 of the 15 subjects did so. Brehm and Cole explained the results by suggesting that in the high importance condition, the favor was given in an inappropriate situation. The inappropriate situation occurred because it was important for the subjects to be free of any obligations created by a favor in order to form an objective impression as instructed by the experimenter.

In this situation the subjects experienced reactance (i.e., reaction to restriction of one's freedom), which is a motivation state "directed toward reestablishment of the loss or threatened freedom" (p. 420). The amount of reactance is a direct function of how important it is for the recipient to be free of any pressures. In Brehm and Cole's study, the subjects in the high importance condition experienced relatively great reactance as a result of receiving a favor and tended not to act as though they were under some pressure to reciprocate. In this way, they were able to reestablish their freedom. Reciprocity under reactance involves much personal cost, and therefore individuals tend not to reciprocate.

The findings by Brehm and Cole (1966) were confirmed by a later study by Schopler and Thompson (1968). In the latter study female subjects were told that the purpose of the experiment was to investigate college females' reactions to presentation of a product (a blouse) by a certain company. The product was presented by a salesman in either a formal or an informal situation. During the interview half of the subjects received a rose, and later all the subjects were asked to volunteer to hand-launder the blouse in a one-week period. As hypothesized, a favor in an informal situation elicited greater reciprocation than a favor in a formal situation. The authors suggested that while in an informal situation, the recipients attributed the favor to the nature of circumstances, in a formal situation the recipients attributed the favor to the donor's own needs. Thus, in the latter condition, the subjects tended not to reciprocate the received favor.

Additional evidence concerning the effect of situational variables on reciprocity behavior was presented by Nemeth (1970a). In her review of studies investigating the bargaining process, she pointed out that these studies reveal little or no reciprocity behavior. She suggested that the lack of reciprocity is due to the inappropriateness of reciprocal acts in the competition paradigm typically used in bargaining studies.

Variables Related to the Culture

Gouldner (1960) suggested that the norm of reciprocity is universal. However, few of the studies carried crosscultural comparisons. In one of the experiments, Gergen et al. (1975) compared reciprocity behavior among college students in the United States, Japan, and Sweden. The results of the study were similar in the three cultures. The subject reciprocated the received help. The reciprocity was higher toward the donor with low personal resources than the one with high personal resources. This experiment generalizes the findings obtained in experiments carried out mostly in the United States.

With regard to subcultural differences among socioeconomic classes, Berkowitz (1966), in a study described in detail in Chapter 4, found that American and English boys from the entrepreneurial middle class and English boys from the working class were reciprocity oriented. That is, they were helpful only after they had received help beforehand. The boys from the bureaucratic middle class were altruistically oriented. They were helpful, disregarding the level of help they had received earlier. In the other two studies, by Muir and Weinstein (1962) done in the United States and by Dreman and Greenbaum (1973) done in Israel it was found that middle-class individuals tend to be reciprocity oriented; they tend rather to exchange help and favors than provide them altruistically.

GENERALIZED RECIPROCITY

A number of studies (e.g., Goranson & Berkowitz, 1966; Greenglass, 1969) have indicated that when the donor disappears after helping the recipient, the recipient is likely to help a person other than the donor. Such behavior may be seen as resulting from generalized obligation to reciprocate and occurring in situations where people are unable to repay their donors. For example, in the study by Goranson and Berkowitz (1966), some subjects were helped by a donor who later left; the subjects were then given an opportunity to help a person other than the donor. The results showed that these subjects who had been previously helped gave more help than other subjects who had not been previously helped. Although it can be argued that generalized reciprocity is altruistic behavior (the recipient helped voluntarily only for the sake of helping), it seems probable that the recipient reduces his feelings of obligation through helping a third person. However, these explanations need to be confirmed by further research.

SUMMARY

The different theories that have explained the basis of reciprocity behavior are in general agreement that the recipient feels an obligation to reciprocate. The model proposed in this chapter explains the decision of the recipient whether or not to reciprocate. The recipient judges the received help or favor by attributing motives to the donor and by calculating the costs and rewards of reciprocity behavior. This judgmental process is affected by variables related to the recipient, variables related to the donor, variables related to the benefit, variables related to the situation, and variables related to the culture.

At this point, there is need for further research for investigating different variables that may affect reciprocity behavior but haven't been investigated yet. Also, contrary to the research concerning altruistic behavior that has been carried out partially in the field, the reciprocity research has been mostly limited to the laboratory. In order to generalize the findings, future research should attempt to also carry out field experiments.

7

COMPENSATORY BEHAVIOR

A compensatory act occurs when a person who has harmed someone later compensates the victim. Harm is defined as behavior that results in some kind of damage to another's property, product, or person (the victim). The compensation act is considered as prosocial behavior to the extent that it is carried out voluntarily for the sake of restitution and without anticipation of external rewards. Under these conditions, it is assumed that the harm-doer intends to correct his previous deed and shows a willingness to be reconciled with the victim. Although harm can be done either intentionally or unintentionally, effecting the reaction of the victim, in both of the cases the compensation may function as a precondition for future interaction between the harm-doer and the victim.

Psychologists attempt to explain the basis of the harm-doer's act of compensation in terms of psychological need. That is, the harm-doer experiences a psychological state of distress and tries to eliminate it. Compensation is only one way of eliminating such distress.

PSYCHOLOGICAL BASIS OF COMPENSATORY BEHAVIOR

Most psychologists agree that the harm-doer experiences distress after harm-doing. There is, however, strong disagreement about the nature of this feeling. Several psychologists (e.g., Freedman, 1970; Rawlings, 1970) have labeled this distress guilt; others (e.g., Bramel, 1969) have called it dissonance; or inequity (e.g., Walster, Berscheid, & Walster, 1970, 1973); and there are some (e.g., Lerner & Matthews, 1967) who have described this distress as a consequence of one's violation of a need to believe in justice.

Guilt

Several psychologists (e.g., Carlsmith & Gross, 1969; Rawlings, 1970) suggested that when a person harms someone, he experiences guilt. Guilt is characterized as an internal feeling of "responsibility and regret" (Freedman, 1970). It is experienced because a harm-doer has done something he considers to be morally wrong and hence deserving of punishment. Guilt feelings are aroused when a person acts in a way that violates moral standards and brought punishment in the past. In this vein, Rawlings (1970) suggested that guilt occurs whenever a harm-doer is aware of a sizeable discrepancy between his act and his internalized values.

It is further thought that individuals who experience guilt look for ways to expiate it. One way to expiate guilt is compensation. A study by Carlsmith and Gross (1969) provides an example of the effect of guilt on compensation. The researchers conducted a study in which each subject was told he was taking part in a learning experiment. In all cases, the subject was the teacher and a confederate played the part of the learner. The subject's job was to press a button whenever the learner made a mistake. For one group of subjects, pressing the button sounded a buzzer and supposedly delivered an electric shock to the learner; for the other group, the button only sounded a buzzer. Thus, half the subjects believed they were doing something unpleasant—shocking another subject. The other half were doing something innocuous—simply signaling when the other person made a mistake. After a series of trials, the experimenter indicated that the study was completed and asked both the subject and the confederate to fill out a short questionnaire. While they were doing this, the confederate turned to the subject and, in a casual way, made the critical request: he asked the subject whether he would be willing to make a series of calls in connection with a campaign to save the California redwood trees. The results indicated that those subjects who thought they had delivered electric shocks were more likely to comply than those who delivered only sounds. It is important to note that the effect was probably not caused by sympathy for someone who had been hurt. In Carlsmith and Gross' study, there was one condition in which subjects did not push the button themselves but watched the confederate receive supposed shocks. There was no difference in compliance between this group and one that merely delivered sounds.

In order to investigate further the relationship between guilt and compensatory behavior Carlsmith, Ellsworth, and Whiteside (reported in Freedman, Carlsmith, & Sears, 1974) explored the effect of confession. One of the common assumptions about confession is that it is "good for the soul," by which we presumably mean that it is a form of expiation. This, in turn, implies that confession should reduce feelings of guilt. If confession does reduce guilt, it should also reduce compensation. In the study, subjects believed they had ruined an experiment because they used information they were not supposed to have had. Some of them were allowed to confess what they had done; others were not given this opportunity; and a third group, who did not think they had ruined the study, served as a control group. The results showed that confessing, which probably reduced guilt, also reduced compensatory behavior. Those in the guilt condition who confessed helped the victim only a little more than those in the control group, but much less than those who did have the opportunity to confess.

Dissonance

Festinger's (1957) theory of cognitive dissonance posited that a person experiences dissonance as a consequence of carrying out behavior that is contrary to his beliefs and values. On this basis Bramel (1969) suggested that when a person harms somebody, he feels dissonance because harm-doing is inconsistent with his expectations about himself. Because he does not usually choose voluntarily to hurt, he is surprised to see himself doing exactly that. A similar explanation was offered by McMillen (1971) and McMillen and Austin (1971). McMillen's interpretation is derived from a recent attempt by Aronson (1969) to clarify dissonance theory. According to Aronson, one of the major determinants of dissonance arousal is whether or not inconsistency exists between an individual's behavior and his self-concept. If an individual possesses a positive self-concept then an act of harm lowers self-esteem; the harm-doer who believes that he is a good person finds himself in a situation of immorality. One of the ways to raise self-esteem again is to compensate the victim.

In order to validate the explanation McMillen (1971) hypothesized that if individuals have an opportunity to bolster their own self-image, then they do not need to compensate in order to raise their self-esteem. In his study, all the subjects were administered a self-esteem test during the first class of the introductory psychology course. Later, the subjects were scheduled to appear in the laboratory in pairs. While they were waiting for the experimenter, a confederate coming for a "forgotten book" told the subjects that he had participated in that experiment the previous day. Moreover, he told them how to answer the particular test given in the experiment. During the experiment the subjects were instructed to take a psychology test in order "to find out how much psychology students know before taking the introductory course" (p. 177). None of the subjects mentioned the fact that somebody had told them the answers to the test. When the subjects completed the test another confederate entered the room. This confederate manipulated the self-esteem: to half of the subjects he showed the results of the self-esteem test given at the beginning of the course; the results were positive and were designed to bolster self-image. At the end of the experiment, the experimenter asked the subjects for help in scoring tests. The results indicated that subjects who "cheated" on the test and then had their self-image bolstered complied less with the request than subjects who "cheated" but whose self-image was not bolstered. This seems to show that compensatory behavior can bolster one's self-esteem, but if other means are available, compensation is not likely to occur.

Inequity

On the basis of Homans' (1961) notion of "distributive justice" and Adams' (1965) theory of "equity," Walster et al. (1970, 1973) have specifically extended the theoretical formulation of equity to harm-doing situations. Thus, Walster et al. (1973) posited that individuals in interactions contribute inputs and receive outcomes. Both inputs and outcomes can have negative and positive values. Individuals who are interacting with each other do generally behave equitably, that is, their profits are more or less equal. However, "when individuals find themselves participating in inequitable relationships, they become distressed. The more inequitable the relationship, the more distressed individuals feel" (p. 153).

In harm-doing situations a harm-doer "commits an act which causes his partner's relative outcomes to fall short of his own" (p. 154). As a result, the harm-doer and the victim find themselves participating in inequitable relationships and the harm-doer experiences distress. Walster et al. suggested that this distress derives from fear of retaliation and/or threatened self-esteem. In order to reduce the distress, the harm-doer attempts to restore equity. One of the ways to restore an equitable relationship is to compensate the victim.

Violation of a Need to Believe in Justice

Lerner's (1970) theory regarding a person's need to believe in a just world also concerns itself with an explanation of the harm-doer's psychological state. Lerner has argued that people strive to maintain their belief in a "just world" in which one gets what one deserves: deserving people are rewarded and the undeserving are appropriately deprived or punished. As Lerner (1970) formulated it,

> It seems that most of the people care deeply about justice for themselves and others—not justice in the legal sense but more basic

notions of justice. We want to believe we live in a world where people get what they deserve, or, rather, deserve what they get. (p. 207)

Thus, causing someone to suffer when the victim has done nothing to merit punishment, threatens the harm-doer's belief in a just world and motivates him to eliminate the unjust suffering by compensating the victim for it.

"Negative State"

Cialdini, Darby, and Vincent (1973) suggested what they called a "parsimonious and integratively powerful" explanation which simply states that "the sight of another's suffering is seen to produce a general, negative affective state, and altruism is seen as but one of several ways a person might go about relieving that state" (p. 505). Thus, a harm-doer who experiences an aversive negative state as a result of his act, attempts to remove this aversive state by compensating the victim. Cialdini considers such compensation altruism, which is characterized as having reinforcing properties. "The personally reinforcing consequences of helping behavior are not seen as pleasant by-products of benevolence but as the prime motive for it" (p. 505).

In an experiment designed to validate the explanation, Cialdini et al. manipulated a situation in which the subjects upset three boxes of computer cards. Later, some of the subjects received a manipulation of negative state relief either by receiving money or approval. In both situations, the goal of the experimenters was to make the subjects feel good in order to relieve their negative aversive state. As dependent variables the experimenters employed two measures. One was the number of phone calls that the harm-doer agreed to make in order to help a student complete a project. The second measure was a dichotomous index of the number of subjects who declined to help versus those who agreed to help. Both of the measures yielded the same results. The subjects who were provided a relief of their negative state through a positive event helped significantly less than the subjects who did not receive relief. Thus, Cialdini et al. concluded that the negative aversive state aroused as a result of harm-doing is a general state. Individuals render help in order to relieve their distress. However, other methods of relieving this distress are also possible.

Need for Cognitive Consistency

Brock (1969) suggested that the compensatory behavior can be explained in terms of "fate control" and maintenance of social consistent behavior. According to Brock,

> An individual who has affected the fate of another person *in a certain magnitude* will repeat that magnitude of control over the other person (or a person in a similar role) if an opportunity to do so presents itself. (p. 143)

This interpretation suggests that an individual who has harmed somebody feels that he affected the fate of the victim. The compensation act also indicates a control of the harm-doer over the victim; the harm-doer initiates the compensation and again affects the fate of the victim.

Brock stated that the perception of self as a consistent individual is crucial for any person. "The socialized individual wants to see himself as behaving consistently toward, as administering comparable treatments to, other persons or classes of other persons" (p. 143). Brock's explanation of compensatory behavior is based on theorizing in social psychology concerning the cognitive consistency needs (e.g., Abelson, Aronson, McGuire, Rosenberg, & Tannenbaum, 1968). These theories postulated that individuals are motivated to act consistently in similar situations.

Summary

Psychologists offered many different explanations to account for the consistently obtained data which indicates that harm-doers tend to compensate their victims. At this point, it is difficult to determine which of the explanations is the correct one. Almost none of the studies measured the psychological state of the harm-doer, and the inference (of a psychological state such as guilt) is based on the interpretation of the researcher. However, all the theories except the one suggested by Brock (1969) assumed that individuals who harm someone experience some kind of distress. This distress was variously labeled guilt, dissonance, inequity, violation of a need to believe in justice, or negative state.

All these theories further assumed that the harm-doer attempted to eliminate his distress and compensation is only one way of eliminating it. Brock's theory about cognitive consistency is the only explanation which does not postulate that the harm-doer experiences an adverse state following the harm-doing act.

VARIABLES AFFECTING COMPENSATORY BEHAVIOR

The most straightforward behavioral reaction of the harm-doer to his misdeed is compensation. Recent studies (e.g., Berscheid & Walster, 1967; Carlsmith & Gross, 1969; Walster & Prestholdt, 1966; Walster, Walster, Abrahams, & Brown, 1966) verify the fact that harm-doers do commonly compensate their victims. After the harm-doing, the transgressors can either initiate the compensatory act themselves when the opportunity arises (e.g., Berscheid & Walster, 1967), or the victim may ask for help and the harm-doer may see this is an opportunity to compensate the victim. Although the harm-doer may react to the victim in a number of ways in order to reduce his distress, Walster et al. (1973) suggested that harm-doers do not tend to have several reactions simultaneously. For example, there is empirical evidence indicating that individuals generally do not use compensation and justification together. Walster and Prestholdt (1966) led social work trainees to inadvertently harm their clients. Subsequently, trainees were asked to volunteer their free time to help these same clients. Compensation and justification responses were found to be negatively related: the more the trainees justified their harm, the less time they volunteered to help the victim.

Few studies have investigated the variables which affect the harm-doer's decision whether or not to compensate the victim. The researchers mostly have investigated situational variables, disregarding other important variables such as personality of the harm-doer, the nature of harm, characteristics of the victim, or cultural norms. This part of the chapter reviews experiments which investigated the effect of situational variables on compensatory behavior.

Presence of the Victim

Some of the evidence suggests that although the harm-doer would like to compensate the victim, he also wants to avoid contact with him. Harm-doers have a tendency to comply less when a request involves associating with the victim than when they need not actually meet the person whom they harmed. A harm-doer seems to have two different motivations. On the one hand, he wants to make up for his harm by helping the victim or by doing something good for someone; on the other hand, he wants to avoid confronting his victim, probably because he is afraid of discovery or embarrassment.

In a study by Freedman, Wallington, and Bless (1967, Experiment II) each subject was brought to a room of a graduate student to fill out a test. In this room, a table was specially prepared so that the slightest touch would tip it over. On the table there was a pile of index cards which had been described as needed for a dissertation. When the subject tipped the table the cards scattered and were mixed. Later, the experimenter made a request. She asked the subjects whether they would be willing to volunteer for an experiment with another person. In one condition a person was described as the graduate student whose cards were scattered and in another condition, the person had no connection with the harm. The results showed that while only 40 percent of the subjects volunteered in the former condition, in the latter 90 percent volunteered. These results clearly indicated that the harm-doers attempted to avoid physical contact with their victims. It is possible that harm-doers would be willing to compensate their victims if the compensation did not involve a face-to-face interaction.

Detection of the Harm

Several studies have suggested that when the harm is undetected, the harm-doers tend not to compensate. Thus, for example, Silverman (1967) exposed sixth-grade children to a situation in which there was temptation to cheat. He then asked the subjects to volunteer for an experiment at a later date, during a free-play period lasting 60 minutes. Analysis of the volunteering data revealed no significant differences between cheaters who were not detected and noncheaters of either sex.

These results are in agreement with those reported by Wallace and Sadalla (1966). In their study, college students were placed in a situation in which the experimenter's confederate suggested tampering with an experimental apparatus which was designed to "blow up" when a specific switch was thrown. The results showed that subjects whose transgression was undetected evidenced no greater willingness to volunteer for another experiment than both subjects who did not transgress and subjects who were not exposed to the temptation. However, subjects whose transgression was detected showed greater willingness to volunteer than other groups of subjects. The authors suggested that the undetected harm-doers tried to avoid further interaction with their victim (i.e., the experimenter) and therefore did not attempt to compensate.

Adequacy of Compensation

Berscheid and Walster (1967) proposed that the harm-doer would be much more likely to perform a compensatory act if it earned an exact compensation than if performance of the act either would be insufficient to make up for the harm done or would confer excessive benefit upon the victim relative to the harm done. The harm-doer would prefer not to make any compensation at all rather than to compensate too little or too much.

In their experiment, Berscheid and Walster instructed the subjects to play a game in which they could win trading stamps. The experimenters manipulated the game in such a way that each subject prevented the victim from winning a prize of two stamp books. During the second game the subjects were assigned to three different conditions. In one condition (insufficient) the subjects were given an opportunity to compensate the victim with three stamps; in the second condition (adequate) the victims received two books and in the third condition (excessive) five books of stamps. The results showed that 42 percent of the subjects compensated in the insufficient condition, 73 percent compensated in the adequate condition, and 61 percent compensated in the excessive condition. Thus, adequacy of compensation appears to be a determinant of a harm-doer's compensatory behavior; individuals tend to compensate their victims if they have an adequate amount of compensation.

Passage of Time

Berscheid, Walster, and Barclay (1969) proposed that the passage of time between the harm-doing and the opportunity to compensate may be an important variable that affects the harm-doer's reaction. Their experiment showed that the passage of a mere five minutes was sufficient to affect the mode of distress reduction. When the harm-doers were provided with an opportunity to perform a compensatory act, and were given little time to consider the extent to which they had violated equity in their relationship with the victim and the ramifications of performing a particular compensatory act, subjects displayed a strong tendency to compensate the victim under insufficient and excessive compensation conditions. However, when the opportunity to compensate the victim was given five minutes after commitment of the harmful act, harm-doers preferred to perform only adequate compensatory acts. These data suggest that if the harm-doer is given time to think about his acts he is less likely to make inadequate or excessive voluntary restitution. During the interval he has an opportunity to think about the implication of inadequate and excessive compensation and to consider other possible ways of reducing his distress.

GENERALIZED COMPENSATION

There is strong evidence indicating that harm-doers comply easily with requests for help even when the request is made by a person other than the victim and it does not benefit the victim. Subjects in several of the experiments were asked to do something that had nothing to do with the person they had injured. In these studies, transgressors complied more than did nontransgressors. This seems to indicate that people can reduce their distress by doing a good deed for someone else. This behavior may be referred to as "generalized compensation."

It is possible to consider generalized compensation as altruistic behavior, because the harm-doer helps someone voluntarily for its own end, not as a result of obligation or quid pro quo. Nevertheless, it can be argued that generalized compensation derives from a harm-doer's need to reduce his distress.

A number of studies have investigated generalized compensation. In a study by Freedman et al. (1967, Experiment I), the experimenter told the subjects that it was extremely important that they not know anything about the test they were going to take, and the situation was set up so that virtually all the subjects said they knew nothing about it. Some of the subjects, however, had been told about the test by a confederate. Thus, these subjects were lying to the experimenter. Later these subjects complied twice as often as other subjects to the request to volunteer for another person's experiment.

In a field experiment by Regan, Williams, and Sparling (1972), a male experimenter asked women in a shopping center to take his picture. The camera was fixed not to work for all of the subjects. For half of the subjects, the experimenter implied that they had broken the camera; the other half were told that the malfunctioning was not their fault. Soon after that, an incident was staged in the shopping center to provide a measure of helping. A female experimenter carrying a broken grocery bag with items falling from it walked in front of the subject. Of the subjects who thought they had broken the camera, 55 percent informed the experimenter that she was losing her groceries; only 15 percent of the subjects in the control group did so.

A similar finding is reported by Brock and Becker (1966). Again, student subjects were induced to press a button that either destroyed the experimenter's apparatus or emitted a slight puff of smoke. Following this, the experimenter asked them to sign a petition advocating doubling tuition at the university. None of the subjects in the low damage condition were willing to sign the petition, while about 50 percent of the subjects in the high-damage condition were willing to sign it.

SUMMARY

The research that has investigated the reaction of the harm-doer after carrying out a transgression is still very limited in scope. Most of the studies have been done in a laboratory and the experimenters have manipulated the harm and the reaction of the harm-doer. The harm-doer therefore cannot choose among the possible responses, being restricted only to the manipulated ones. In some of the studies, the harm-doer was able to compensate the victim; in others he could only help someone other than his victim. In other studies, the behavioral reactions were blocked and the harm-doer could only react psychologically. Thus, despite the existence of a substantial body of research, surprisingly little is known about the conditions that foster a specific behavior following a specific act of harm-doing. This relative paucity of experimentally derived data is in part attributable to the obvious difficulties involved in arranging laboratory conditions for the study of harm-doing.

Many of these experiments were designed very carefully to eliminate the possibility of experimental artifacts, primarily by keeping the person who request the altruistic behavior blind as to the subject's experimental condition. Nevertheless, in all cases the subjects were college students who knew that they were participating in a psychological experiment. Perhaps when people know that they are participating in an experiment, they feel that they are being scrutinized and evaluated by a psychologist and thus act in a specific manner. Harm-doing is both particularly damaging to self-esteem and especially likely to lead to a high degree of motivation to demonstrate to others connected with the situation that one is, after all, a worthwhile person.

Because most of the research has been done in a laboratory, it was difficult to manipulate different types of harm. Almost all the experiments used either unintentional harm or harm of a coerced nature. Thus, the conclusions drawn from these studies are limited in scope. It would be important to compare the reactions of an intentional harm-doer and an unintentional harm-doer. It would be especially valuable to study the psychological state of an intentional harm-doer after a transgression; for example, does he feel guilt?

Systematic examination of the variables related to the occurrence of compensation or other reactions has been hindered by the nature of those theories that seek to explain the psychological state of the harm-doer after a transgression. As a result of this direction, many variables received no attention by researchers. It is reasonable to assume that the reaction of the harm-doer is determined by his personality variables; situational variables (e.g., presence of others, previous behavioral example, prior harming, etc.); type of relationship the harm-doer has with his victim (e.g., friendship, acquaintanceship, etc.); and the characteristics of the victim (e.g., sex, age, race, etc.). Finally, the reactions of the harm-doer depend on the prevailing norms within the harm-doer's group. Each of these types of variables should be investigated as to its influence on the harm-doer's reaction.

Although most of the research in the area of harm-doing is aimed at determining the psychological state of the harm-doer, the results are not perfectly clear. There do seem to be specific psychological states produced in a person by harm-doing, which are often labeled guilt or dissonance. But in virtually all the published laboratory research, there was no measure of the manipulation that aimed to produce such a state. In order to come to a fuller understanding of the psychological state, it may be necessary in future experimentation to attempt to more systematically tap the content of this psychological state produced by manipulation. Regan (1971) did attempt to measure mood by means of general semantic differential scales, and she found that subjects who harmed reported themselves as more upset than either of the other two groups (i.e., the control group and those subjects who were witness to the harm-doing). More detailed self-ratings might be helpful in the future.

In summary, it can be concluded that with the difficulties in generalizing from the laboratory to the field, with the relatively narrow focus of the experiments conducted so far, and with the multitude of apparently uncorrelated reactions of the harm-doer, any generalizations are tenuous at best. More research is necessary in order to more fully understand the compensatory behavior of the harm-doer.

8

PROSOCIAL BEHAVIOR: CONCLUSIONS

CHARACTERISTICS OF THE STUDIES

The studies that have investigated prosocial behavior have four characteristics in common; use of experimentation, use of strangers as subjects, investigations of antecedents, and investigation of one particular act.

Use of Experimentation

First, the investigation of prosocial behavior was carried out primarily (except for two or three studies) through research methods of experimentation. Most of the experiments were carried out in laboratories and few were carried out in the "real world."

With the growing criticism of the experimentation method (see Adair, 1973, for an extensive review) it has been suggested that prosocial behavior can also be investigated by other methods. Following McGuire's (1973) proposal, prosocial behavior can be studied through interviews, content analysis, questionnaires, and even observations. The use of various techniques can extend the generalization of the experimental findings across different situations and populations.

Use of Strangers

Second, almost all the experiments of prosocial behavior studied behaviors of strangers. That is, in experiments investigating altruistic behavior, strangers asked the subjects for help, and in experiments investigating restitution, the subjects were provided with help by strangers, or they were induced to harm strangers. The method of using subjects who are strangers differs considerably from the quality of other interpersonal relationships. It is obvious that in relationships like friendship, family, or acquaintanceship people help each other and harm each other. However, very little research has investigated prosocial reactions among individuals who are not strangers. Possibly different rules govern interactions between friends than between strangers. Further research must clarify whether such differences exist and the nature of these differences.

Investigation of Antecedents

The third common characteristic of the studies of prosocial behavior is that almost all of them attempted to determine the antecedent conditions of this behavior. That is, the experimenters have investigated those variables which may increase or decrease the likelihood of prosocial acts. The researchers have focused mainly on situational conditions and personal variables. The former included characteristics of the situation and temporary psychological states of the actors, while the latter focus on the personality and the demographic variables of the subjects.

Examples of some of the situational variables are

1. Observation of a model (e.g., Rosenhan & White, 1967)
2. Mood of the subjects (e.g., Isen & Levin, 1972)
3. Observation of altruistic behavior (e.g., Macaulay, 1970)
4. Presence of others (e.g., Goodstadt, 1971)
5. Compliance with previous requests (Freedman & Fraser, 1966)
6. Degree of dependency of the person in need (e.g., Berkowitz & Daniels, 1964)

7. Prior help received (e.g., Goranson & Berkowitz, 1966)
8. Amount of freedom the helping person has in deciding whether to help or not to help (e.g., Jones, 1970)
9. Adequacy of compensation (e.g., Berscheid & Walster, 1967)
10. Observation of harm doing (e.g., Regan, 1971)

The researchers have also studied personal antecedents, although the focus has mainly been on demographic variables. Thus, the studies have investigated who is more likely to carry out prosocial reactions and who is more likely to receive help or assistance. Psychologists have studied such personal variables as

1. Race (e.g., Bryan & Test, 1967)
2. Sex (e.g., Gruder & Cook, 1971)
3. Age (e.g., Lowe & Ritchey, 1973)
4. Social class (e.g., Berkowitz & Friedman, 1967)
5. Social responsibility (e.g., Berkowitz & Daniels, 1964)

As can be seen, psychologists have devoted much effort to compiling a list of variables which have an effect on prosocial behavior. Such a list can be extended and new variables will probably be added. However, the research should also focus on the cognitive process which determines whether a person will engage in a prosocial act. At present, there are a number of theories (e.g., Latané & Darley, 1970; Piliavin & Piliavin, 1972) that attempt to describe the process of decision making in which the potential helper engages and offer a description of the cognitive process of such decision making. However, these theories are at best serving as hypotheses and future research should attempt to validate them.

Investigation of One Act

The fourth common characteristic of the studies done in the area of prosocial behavior is the isolation of one specific act. The experimenters have created a situation either in a laboratory or in the field to elicit a specific prosocial act. The act could be altruism, reciprocity, or compensation. Thus, the investigators studied the antecedents of an altruistic act separately from the reaction of the recipient. The reciprocal behavior has usually been induced by using a confederate who had been helping the recipient, and the reaction of a harm-doer has been studied after the harm has been manipulated by the experimenter.

It seems that in order to understand the mechanisms of prosocial behavior, in order to suggest new directions for research, and in order to better understand the situational and personal conditions involved, we ought to analyze these behaviors using the holistic approach. Thus, in studying altruistic acts we should also look at the reaction of the recipient, which is dependent on the behavior of the donor. We should look at the behavior of both the donor and recipient at the same time. Harré and Secord (1972) posited that psychologists must examine the entire "episode" in which the behavior is seen—"any sequence of happenings in which human beings engage which has some principle of unity" (p. 10) must be studied as a whole. Component acts lose their meaning when taken from an entire "episode."

In the last section of the book, a new framework for prosocial behavior was proposed. This framework suggests viewing prosocial behavior as sequences of two interactions and takes the holistic approach in analyzing prosocial behavior.

THE FRAMEWORK OF PROSOCIAL BEHAVIOR

It is suggested that prosocial behavior can be viewed as consisting of a sequence of two specific types of interactions. Each interaction can be seen as an "episode." The first type of interaction describes the sequence of happenings between a donor and a recipient. The second one describes the sequence of acts between a harm-doer and a victim. The former will be called "giving interaction" and the second will be called "harm-doing interaction."

Giving Interaction

The giving interaction describes the intercourse between the donor (D) and the recipient (R) (Figure 4). The whole sequence

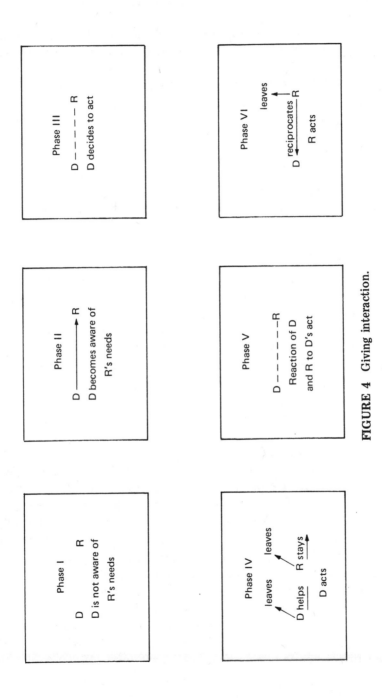

FIGURE 4 Giving interaction.

will be divided into six phases. Each phase will be described and analyzed by illustrations taken from studies done in this area.

Phase I: Unawareness of R's Needs

Phase I is the starting point in the analysis of the sequence of giving. Person D is not aware of R's needs. It does not mean that D and R don't have any relationship. It might be that D and R are close friends who interact often, but at this point D doesn't know that R has a need for something. Of course, a simpler example might be a case where D doesn't know R and doesn't have any contact with him. In either case, he is unaware of R's needs.

Phase II: Awareness

In this phase, D becomes aware of R's needs. D can become aware in different ways; R can come to D and ask for help or D can notice R's needs. Various investigators employed different techniques. In some studies, R's needs were made obvious, thus D passing by had to notice R's needs; for example, in Bryan and Test (1967) R was placed beside a car with a flat tire. In some studies (e.g., Aderman, 1972), a third person made D aware of R's situation; for example, in Goodstadt's (1971) study, a secretary presented the subject with the information that R needed help. In other studies, D had no actual contact with R; Hornstein, Fisch, and Holmes (1968) employed a manipulation in which D found a lost wallet, never having contact with R. Sometimes R made a direct request for a favor from D, notifying D that he needed some help (e.g., Gaertner & Bickman, 1971); for example, in Gaertner's (1973) study, D asked R to call a garage for him. In many experiments (e.g., Bickman, 1971), D becomes aware of R's needs when R cries for help without referring to anybody in particular.

The awareness phase is important because it may determine what course of action will be taken by D. Several studies indicate that sometimes it may make a difference for D if he is directly asked for help by R, or if he notices R's state without any direct request. For example, Berkowitz (1969) found that a person asking for assistance was more disliked than the person not directly requesting help, presumably because the request for help restricted the subject's behavioral freedom. He felt pressure to give aid to the person and did not feel he had the personal freedom to make the decision.

Another important factor in Phase II is the manner in which the request is made. For example, Horowitz (1968) demonstrated that it makes a difference if the request is made in such a way that D feels that he has the choice either to help or refuse. It would be useful to study the different ways in which people become aware of another's needs in order to find the most efficient methods not only to make D aware but also most willing to provide assistance or grant a favor.

Phase III: Decision Making

Phase III is the stage in which D has to decide what to do. At this point, when D acknowledges R's needs, he may decide either to ignore the needs and not help or he may decide to offer assistance. When he decides to help, he has to determine in which way and how much help he is willing to provide.

The decision-making process depends on D's familiarity with the situation. The more experienced D is with the situation, the easier it will be for him to decide what to do. Facing a beggar who asks for a dime is different than seeing a person fall in the street. D has probably faced the first situation many times; therefore it will take him a shorter time to decide what to do since the reaction to it is almost automatic. Since D might be facing the second situation for the first time, the decision process will be more of a conscious one. Second, it is proposed that the decision process involves two basic judgments: (a) the attribution process: why the person is in need, and (b) the calculation of the costs-rewards involved in helping. In emergency situations the judgmental process is preceded by physiological arousal and the judgmental process itself also involves labeling of the situation. The judgments are affected by four types of variables:

1. Personal variables of D, which include his disposition, traits, and demographic characteristics
2. Situational variables, which include the temporary psychological state of D and the characteristics of the situation

3. Characteristics of the person in need (R), especially the characteristics which are externally salient such as sex, physical attractiveness, and race
4. Cultural variables, which include norms and values prevailing within society

As was noted, most of the studies in the area of prosocial behavior have looked at the variables which affect D's decision to carry out an altruistic act. Researchers have examined the conditions under which people are likely to carry out altruistic behavior, but they rarely study the conditions under which people decide not to help. It seems that this kind of research could be equally important in order to understand the prosocial behavior.

Phase IV: D's Act

D may decide not to help and leave the field, D may help R and leave the field, or D may help and stay in contact with R. The focus in this phase is on D's behavior. The questions that should be studied are: how D leaves the field if he decides not to help, how he helps, what type of an altruistic act he performs, and when and/or how he maintains contact with R. The first and last questions are neglected by the researchers. Psychologists have almost ignored the conditions under which refusal to help occur. How does the person rationalize his refusal of help? What kinds of cognitions are used? Does he feel compelled to offer an excuse to D, and if he does, how is it done? All these questions remain unanswered and indicate possible future directions for research.

Most of the studies have emphasized the quantitative aspect of help. For example, the number of boxes the person completed (e.g., Berkowitz & Daniels, 1964; Goranson & Berkowitz, 1966), the number of hours a person volunteered for an experiment (e.g., Horowitz, 1968; Jones, 1970), or the number of questionnaires stapled for the experimenter (e.g., Gruder & Cook, 1971). Other experiments employed as a dependent variable the number of subjects willing or unwilling to help (e.g., Bryan & Test, 1967).

Either providing positive reinforcement to a person in need or withdrawing negative reinforcement can be an altruistic act. In the first case, D can give a dime, make boxes, or volunteer for an experiment. In the latter case, one person can relieve another's pain or distress. In experiments which have studied helping in an emergency, subjects attempted to relieve someone's pain. These experiments employed two kinds of dependent measures:

1. How the person helps
2. How long it takes him to do so

These studies distinguished between direct help: actually helping the victim, and indirect help: calling another person in order to report the emergency or administer assistance. The conditions under which people react in either way should be investigated.

Another problem related to this phase is whether the donor leaves the field or stays in contact with the recipient. This is an important factor for the recipient as will be indicated in the analysis of the next phase.

Phase V: Reaction of D and R

Few experiments have studied the reaction of the donor after carrying out the altruistic act. The emphasis has been on the decision to help, but it also would be important to study the donor's reaction toward the recipient and his attitude toward himself and the act. One of the few studies which investigated the reaction of the donor after providing help was done by Freedman and Fraser (1966). They suggested that subjects who performed one altruistic favor may change their perceptions and see themselves as "activists"; this change in self perception may cause a donor to be more likely to perform altruistic acts for others in the future.

A wide range of studies have focused on the recipient's reaction toward the donor. The research that has studied the reaction of the recipient derives mostly from the Gouldner (1960) postulate about the presence of the norm of reciprocity. According to Gouldner's reasoning, reciprocity implies the internalization of a norm that obliges a recipient to repay his donor.

Most of the studies have focused on those situations where the recipient decides to make restitution by benefiting his donor in return for the help or favor he had previously received. During this phase, the recipient must decide what kind of reciprocity he will provide and how he will provide it. The decision of the recipient is based on two judgments:

1. The recipient's attribution of the donor's motives
2. The recipient's calculation of costs-rewards involved in reciprocity behavior

This judgmental process is affected by five types of variables:

1. Variables related to the characteristics of the recipient
2. Variables related to the characteristics and behaviors of the donor
3. Variables related to the benefit itself
4. Variables related to the situation in which the donor helped the recipient
5. Cultural variables

Phase VI: R's Act

As was pointed out, R (the recipient) may leave the field, or he may reciprocate the help he received. The experiments manipulated the reciprocity behavior in different ways, providing the recipient with the opportunity to reciprocate. The recipient may benefit the donor by providing positive reinforcement to him or by withdrawing negative reinforcement. It may make a difference for the recipient if he is asked for help by his donor or if he himself initiates the reciprocal act.

In most of the experiments, psychologists employed quantitative measures of reciprocity. Kahn and Tice (1973) used two measures: the degree of difficulty of the task the recipient selected, and the number of credits assigned for the donor's finished product. Nacci, Stapleton and Tedeschi (1973) measured the frequency with which recipients returned benefits and the absolute amount of rewards given to the donor. In the Nemeth (1970b) study, the donor asked the recipient for a favor (to help to fill out questionnaire surveys).

Although most of the studies have structured reciprocity in terms of tangible rewards, there are additional ways of repaying a debt. For example, in the Bar-Tal and Greenberg (1974) and Greenglass (1969) experiments, the dependent measure of reciprocity consisted of the number of points that the recipient assigned as an evaluation of the donor's "motivation to work."

Summary

In summary, the interaction of giving consists of two acts: D's altruistic act, and R's act of reciprocity. The former is the necessary condition for the latter but not a sufficient one, under many circumstances, we witness only the altruistic act. Both of the acts are positive forms of social behavior. In both cases the person benefits another but there are different motivations underlying each behavior. It should be emphasized, however, that the act of helping which is performed with clear expectations of reciprocity is not included within the framework of prosocial behavior. This kind of behavior is based on the premise that individuals interact socially because of the rewards they think these relationships will bring, and continue interacting because of the rewards other people provide (Blau, 1964; Homans, 1961). Although externally derived incentives are important determinants of behavior, there is probably a far greater incidence of altruistic action than one might expect.

Harm-doing Interaction

The harm-doing interaction between the harm-doer (H) and the victim (V) consists of five phases, but only the last two are considered positive forms of social behavior and even these require very specific behaviors to qualify to this category (Figure 5).

This analysis will partially ignore the first three phases of the interaction, because they deal only with the negative forms of behavior: harm-doing. The positive forms of social behavior can

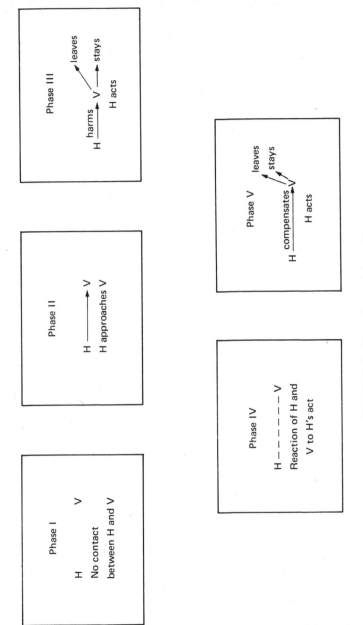

FIGURE 5 Harm-doing interaction.

occur in the last phase of the interaction, only when the harm-doer decides to compensate the victim.

Phase I: No Interaction

Phase I is the starting point in the sequence of events. II is not interacting with R. They may be known to one another but in this phase there is no contact between them.

Phases II and III: Approach and Aggression

H can approach V with or without the intention to harm him. H can harm R and leave the field, or he may stay in contact with him. These two phases, which deal with aggressive behavior, will be discussed here.

Phase IV: Reaction of Harm-doer

The positive term of social behavior consists of the compensation the harm-doer provides in order to make restitution. After harming the victim, the harm-doer feels distress (Brock & Buss, 1962; Lerner & Matthews, 1967; Regan, 1971). Different theories (e.g., Rawlings, 1970; Walster, Berscheid, & Walster, 1973) attempt to explain the nature of this distress and a number of studies (e.g., Berscheid & Walster, 1967) have investigated the variables which may affect the decision of the harm-doer to compensate the victim. Few of the studies have investigated the reaction of the victim, and further research should determine the relationship between the reaction of the victim and the reaction of the harm-doer.

Phase V: P's Act

In many studies (e.g., Darlington & Macker, 1966; Freedman, Wallington, & Bless, 1967; Regan, Williams, & Sparling, 1972), the experimenters blocked compensation routes for the harm-doers but provided an opportunity to help someone other than the victim. For example, in the Darlington and Macker study, persons who believed they had harmed someone else were relatively quick to agree to donate blood to a local hospital. In an experiment by Carlsmith and Gross (1969), the more the subjects thought they had hurt their partner earlier, the more they eventually tried to make up for it by complying with the request to aid an ecology group.

Very few experiments (e.g., Berscheid & Walster, 1967; Berscheid, Walster, & Barclay, 1969) have studied the direct compensation to the victim by the harm doer. This behavior requires more extensive research in order to determine the conditions under which the person chooses to compensate his victim and how he does it.

In most of the harm-doing studies, the harm was manipulated by the experimenter, who made the subjects believe that they had harmed somebody. This was usually unintentional harming and therefore the willingness to carry out an altruistic act was great in order to make up for the harm. It would be important to study also the reaction of the intentional harm-doer and the condition under which he will attempt to compensate his victim.

SUMMARY

The proposed framework analyzes the interaction between the donor and the recipient and between the harm-doer and the victim in a sequence of happenings which consist of two episodes. One episode describes the giving interaction between the donor and the recipient, the second episode describes the harm-doing interaction between the harm-doer and the victim. This framework views the acts of altruism, reciprocity, and compensation as a sequence of behaviors. Such a holistic view facilitates an understanding of the interpersonal behavior of individuals participating in the interactions. As a result, the analysis derived from the framework indicated that the research of prosocial behavior disregarded some important issues related to the giving and the harm-doing interactions. These neglected issues were raised through the description of the new framework and suggest new directions for research.

The area of prosocial behavior is a relatively new one in social psychology. Much research is needed to clarify the dynamics of prosocial behavior. This research is especially important since the theories and findings of prosocial behavior can be applied to other practical fields such as social work, nursing, education, etc. These helping professions hopefully will be able to utilize the accumulated knowledge about prosocial behavior.

In addition, understanding prosocial behavior could be functional in improving the quality of life. The more people share, help, reciprocate, and compensate, the better interpersonal relationships will be among human beings. This might be personal bias, but the research of prosocial behavior hopefully will help us understand the conditions under which the number of altruists could increase.

REFERENCES

Abelson, R. P., Aronson, E., McGuire, W. J., Newcomb, T. M., Rosenberg, M. J., & Tannenbaum, P. H. (Eds.). *Theories of cognitive consistency: A sourcebook.* Chicago: Rand McNally, 1968.

Adair, J. G. *The human subject: The social psychology of the psychological experiment.* Boston: Little, Brown & Co., 1973.

Adams, J. S. Inequity in social exchange. In L. Berkowitz (Ed.), *Advances in experimental social psychology* (Vol. 2). New York: Academic Press, 1965.

Aderman, D. Elation, depression, and helping behavior. *Journal of Personality and Social Psychology*, 1972, *24*, 91–101.

Allport, G. W., Vernon, P. E., & Lindzey, G. *A study of values.* Boston: Houghton Mifflin, 1960.

Aronfreed, J. *Conduct and conscience: The socialization of internalized control over behavior.* New York: Academic Press, 1968.

Aronfreed, J. The socialization of altruistic and sympathetic behavior: Some theoretical and experimental analyses. In J. Macaulay & L. Berkowitz (Eds.), *Altruism and helping behavior.* New York: Academic Press, 1970.

Aronson, E. The theory of cognitive dissonance: A current perspective. In L. Berkowitz (Ed.), *Advances in experimental social psychology* (Vol. 4). New York: Academic Press, 1969.

Baer, D. M., & Sherman, J. A. Reinforcement control of generalized imitation in young children. *Journal of Experimental Child Psychology*, 1964, *1*, 37–49.

Bandura, A. Vicarious processes: A case of no trial learning. In L. Berkowitz (Ed.), *Advances in social psychology* (Vol. 2). New York: Academic Press, 1965.

Bandura, A. *Principles of behavior modification.* New York: Holt, Rinehart & Winston, 1969.

Bandura, A. *Social learning theory.* New York: General Learning Press, 1971.

Bandura, A., & Walters, R. *Social learning and personality development.* New York: Holt, Rinehart & Winston, 1963.

Barnett, M. A., & Bryan, J. H. Effects of competition with outcome feedback on children's helping behavior. *Developmental Psychology*, 1974, *10*, 838-842.

Baron, R. A. Behavioral effects of interpersonal attraction: Compliance with requests from liked and disliked others. *Psychonomic Science*, 1971, *25*, 325-326.

Baron, R. A., Byrne, D., & Griffitt, W. *Social psychology: Understanding human interaction.* Boston: Allyn & Bacon, 1974.

Bar-Tal, D., & Greenberg, M. S. *Indebtedness as a motive for exposure to and learning of information.* Paper presented at the meeting of the Eastern Psychological Association, Washington, D.C., May 1973.

Bar-Tal, D., & Greenberg, M. S. Effect of passage of time on reactions to help and harm. *Psychological Reports*, 1974, *34*, 617-618.

Bar-Tal, D., Harmon, M., & Greenberg, M. *Effect of relationship between donor and recipient, and harm-doer and victim on reciprocity.* Unpublished manuscript, University of Pittsburgh, 1975.

Berkowitz, L. *Aggression: A social psychological analysis.* New York: McGraw-Hill, 1962.

Berkowitz, L. A laboratory investigation of social class and national differences in helping behavior. *International Journal of Psychology*, 1966, *1*, 231-242.

Berkowitz, L. Resistance to improper dependency relationships. *Journal of Experimental Social Psychology*, 1969, *5*, 283-294.

Berkowitz, L. Social norms, feelings, and other factors affecting helping and altruism. In L. Berkowitz (Ed.), *Advances in experimental social psychology* (Vol. 6). New York: Academic Press, 1972.

Berkowitz, L. Reactance and the unwillingness to help others. *Psychological Bulletin*, 1973, *79*, 310–317.

Berkowitz, L. *A survey of social psychology*. Hinsdale, Ill.: The Dryden Press, 1975.

Berkowitz, L., & Connor, W. H. Success, failure and social responsibility. *Journal of Personality and Social Psychology*, 1966, *4*, 664–669.

Berkowitz, L., & Daniels, L. R. Responsibility and dependency. *Journal of Abnormal and Social Psychology*, 1963, *66*, 429–436.

Berkowitz, L., & Daniels, L. R. Affecting the salience of the social responsibility norm: Effect of past help on the response to dependency relationships. *Journal of Abnormal and Social Psychology*, 1964, *68* 275–281.

Berkowitz, L., & Friedman, P. Some social class differences in helping behavior. *Journal of Personality and Social Psychology*, 1967, *5*, 217–225.

Berscheid, E., & Walster, E. When does a harm-doer compensate a victim? *Journal of Personality and Social Psychology*, 1967, *6*, 435–441.

Berscheid, E., Walster, E., & Barclay, A. Effect of time on tendency to compensate a victim. *Psychological Reports*, 1969, *25*, 431–436.

Bickman, L. The effect of another bystander's ability to help on bystander intervention in an emergency. *Journal of Experimental Social Psychology*, 1971, *7*, 367–379.

Bickman, L. Social influence and diffusion of responsibility in an emergency. *Journal of Experimental Social Psychology*, 1972, *8*, 438–445.

Bickman, L., & Kamzan, M. The effect of race and need on helping behavior. *Journal of Social Psychology*, 1973, *89*, 73–77.

Blau, P. M. *Exchange and power in social life*. New York: Wiley, 1964.

Borofsky, F. L., Stollak, G. E., & Messé, L. A. Sex differences in bystander reactions to physical assault. *Journal of Experimental Social Psychology*, 1971, *7*, 313–318.

Bramel, D. Interpersonal attraction, hostility, and perception. In J. Mills (Ed.), *Experimental social psychology*. New York: Macmillan, 1969.

Brehm, J. W., & Cole, A. H. Effect of a favor which reduces freedom. *Journal of Personality and Social Psychology*, 1966, *3*, 420–426.

Brock, T. C. On interpreting the effects of transgression upon compliance. *Psychological Bulletin*, 1969, *72*, 138–145.

Brock, T. C., & Becker, L. A. "Debriefing" and susceptibility to subsequent experimental manipulations. *Journal of Experimental Social Psychology*, 1966, *2*, 314–323.

Brock, T. C., & Buss, A. H. Dissonance, aggression, and evaluation of pain. *Journal of Abnormal and Social Psychology*, 1962, *65*, 197–202.

Bryan, J. H. Model affect and children's imitative altruism. *Child Development*, 1971, *42*, 2061–2065.

Bryan, J. H. Why children help: A review. *Journal of Social Issues*, 1972, *28*(3), 87–104.

Bryan, J. H., Redfield, J., & Mader, S. Words and deeds about altruism and the subsequent reinforcement power of the model. *Child Development*, 1971, *42*, 1501–1508.

Bryan, J. H., & Test, M. A. Models and helping: Naturalistic studies in aiding behavior. *Journal of Personality and Social Psychology*, 1967, *6*, 400–407.

Bryan, J. H., & Walbek, N. H. The impact of words and deeds concerning altruism upon children. *Child Development*, 1970, *41*, 747–757. (a)

Bryan, J. H., & Walbek, N. H. Preaching and practicing generosity: Children's actions and reactions. *Child Development*, 1970, *41*, 329–353. (b)

Buss, A. H. *The psychology of aggression.* New York: Wiley, 1961.

Byrne, D. E. *The attraction paradigm.* New York: Academic Press, 1971.

Campbell, D. T. Ethnocentric and other altruistic motives. In D. Levine (Ed.), *Nebraska Symposium on Motivation* (Vol. 13). Lincoln: University of Nebraska Press, 1965.

Campbell, D. T. On the genetics of altruism and the counter-hedonic components in human culture. *Journal of Social Issues*, 1972, *28*(3), 21–37.

Carlsmith, J. M., & Gross, A. E. Some effects of guilt on compliance. *Journal of Personality and Social Psychology*, 1969, *11*, 232–239.

Cialdini, R. B., Darby, B. L., & Vincent, J. E. Transgression and altruism: A case for hedonism. *Journal of Experimental Social Psychology*, 1973, *9*, 502–516.

Cialdini, R. B., Vincent, J. E., Lewis, S. K., Catalan, J., Wheeler, D., & Darby, B. L. Reciprocal concessions procedure for inducing compliance: The door-in-the-face technique. *Journal of Personality and Social Psychology*, 1975, *31*, 206–215.

Clark, R. D. Effects of sex and race on helping behavior in a nonreactive setting. *Representative Research in Social Psychology*, 1974, *5* 1–6.

Clark, R. D., & Word, L. E. Why don't bystanders help? Because of ambiguity? *Journal of Personality and Social Psychology*, 1972, *24*, 392–400.

Cohen, R. Altruism: Human, cultural, or what? *Journal of Social Issues*, 1972, *28*(3), 39–57.

Crandall, B. D., Crandall, V. J., & Patkovsky, W. A. A children's social desirability questionnaire. *Journal of Consulting Psychology*, 1965, *29*, 27–36.

Darley, J. M., & Batson, C. D. "From Jerusalem to Jericho": A study of situational and dispositional variables in helping behavior. *Journal of Personality and Social Psychology*, 1973, *27*, 100–108.

Darley, J. M., & Latané, B. Bystander intervention in emergencies: Diffusion of responsibility. *Journal of Personality and Social Psychology*, 1968, *8*, 377–383.

Darley, J. M., & Latané, B. Norms and normative behavior: Field studies of social interdependence. In J. Macauley & L. Berkowitz (Eds.), *Altruism and helping behavior*. New York: Academic Press, 1970.

Darley, J. M., Teger, A. I., & Lewis, L. D. Do groups always inhibit individuals' responses to potential emergencies? *Journal of Personality and Social Psychology*, 1973, *26*, 395–399.

Darlington, R. B., & Macker, C. E. Displacement of guilt-produced altruistic behavior. *Journal of Personality and Social Psychology*, 1966, *4*, 442–443.

Doland, D. M., & Adelberg, K. The learning of sharing behavior. *Child Development*, 1967, *38*, 695–700.

Dollard, J., Miller, N. E., Doob, L. W., Mowrer, O. H., & Sears, R. R. *Frustration and aggression.* New Haven: Yale University Press, 1939.

Dovidio, J. F., & Morris, W. M. Effects of stress and commonality of fate on helping behavior. *Journal of Personality and Social Psychology*, 1975, *31*, 145–149.

Dreman, S. B., & Greenbaum, C. W. Altruism or reciprocity: Sharing behavior in Israeli kindergarten children. *Child Development*, 1973, *44*, 61–68.

Elliott, R. E., & Vasta, R. The modeling of sharing: Effects associated with vicarious reinforcement, symbolization, age, and generalization. *Journal of Experimental Child Psychology*, 1970, *10*, 8–15.

Emler, N. P., & Rushton, J. P. Cognitive-developmental factors in children's generosity. *British Journal of Social and Clinical Psychology*, 1974, *13*, 277–281.

Emswiller, T., Deaux, K., & Willits, J. E. Similarity, sex, and requests for small favors. *Journal of Applied Social Psychology*, 1971, *1*, 284–291.

Endler, N. S. The person versus the situation—a pseudo issue? A response to Alker. *Journal of Personality*, 1973, *41*, 287–303.

Feldman, R. E. Response to compatriot and foreigner who seek assistance. *Journal of Personality and Social Psychology*, 1968, *10*, 202–214.

Festinger, L. *A theory of cognitive dissonance.* Evanston, Ill.: Row, Peterson, 1957.

Fischer, W. F. Sharing in preschool children as a function of amount and type of reinforcement. *Genetic Psychology Monographs*, 1963, *68*, 215–245.

Freedman, J. L. Transgression, compliance, and guilt. In J. R. Macaulay & L. Berkowitz (Eds.), *Altruism and helping behavior.* New York: Academic Press, 1970.

Freedman, J. L., Carlsmith, J. M., & Sears, D. O. *Social psychology.* (2nd ed.). Englewood Cliffs, N.J.: Prentice-Hall, 1974.

Freedman, J. L., & Fraser, S. C. Compliance without pressure:

The foot-in-the-door technique. *Journal of Personality and Social Psychology*, 1966, *4*, 195–202.

Freedman, J. W., Wallington, S. A., & Bless, E. Compliance without pressure: The effect of guilt. *Journal of Personality and Social Psychology*, 1967, 7, 117–124.

Gaertner, S. L. Helping behavior and racial discrimination among liberals and conservatives. *Journal of Personality and Social Psychology*, 1973, *25*, 335–341.

Gaertner, S., & Bickman, L. Effects of race on the elicitation of helping behavior: The wrong numbers technique. *Journal of Personality and Social Psychology*, 1971, *20*, 218–222.

Gergen, K. J., Ellsworth, P., Maslach, C., & Seipel, M. Obligation, donor, resources, and reactions to aid in three cultures. *Journal of Personality and Social Psychology*, 1975, *31*, 390–400.

Gergen, K. J., Gergen, J. M., & Meter, K. Individual orientations to prosocial behavior. *Journal of Social Issues*, 1972, *28*(3), 105–130.

Gewirtz, J. L., & Stingle, K. C. The learning of generalized imitation as the basis for identification. *Psychological Review*, 1968, *75*, 374–397.

Goodstadt, M. S. Helping and refusal to help: A test of balance and reactance theories. *Journal of Experimental Social Psychology*, 1971, 7, 610–622.

Goranson, R. E., & Berkowitz, L. Reciprocity and responsibility reactions to prior help. *Journal of Personality and Social Psychology*, 1966, *3*, 227–232.

Gouldner, A. W. The norm of reciprocity: A preliminary statement. *American Sociological Review*, 1960, *25*, 161–178.

Graf, R. C., & Riddell, L. C. Helping behavior as a function of interpersonal perception. *Journal of Social Psychology*, 1972, *86*, 227–231.

Green, F. P., & Schneider, F. W. Age differences in the behavior of boys on three measures of altruism. *Child Development*, 1974, *45*, 248–251.

Greenberg, M. S. *A preliminary statement on a theory of indebtedness.* Paper presented at the meeting of the Western Psychological Association, San Diego, March 1968.

Greenberg, M. S. A theory of indebtedness. In K. Gergen, M. S. Greenberg, & R. H. Willis (Eds.), *Social exchange: Advances in theory and research.* New York: Wiley, in press.

Greenberg, M. S., Block, M. W., & Silverman, M. A. Determinants of helping behavior: Person's rewards versus other's costs. *Journal of Personality*, 1971, *39*, 79-93.

Greenberg, M. S., & Frisch, D. M. Effect of intentionality on willingness to reciprocate a favor. *Journal of Experimental Social Psychology*, 1972, *8*, 99-111.

Greenberg, M. S., & Shapiro, S. P. Indebtedness: An adverse aspect of asking for and receiving help. *Sociometry*, 1971, *34*, 290-301.

Greenglass, E. R. Effects of prior help and hindrance on willingness to help another: Reciprocity or social responsibility. *Journal of Personality and Social Psychology*, 1969, *11*, 224-231.

Gross, A. E., Wallston, B. S., & Piliavin, I. M. Beneficiary attractiveness and cost as determinants of responses to routine requests for help. *Sociometry*, 1975, *38*, 131-140.

Gruder, C. L., & Cook, T. D. Sex, dependency, and helping. *Journal of Personality and Social Psychology*, 1971, *19*, 290-294.

Grusec, J. E. Demand characteristics of the modeling experiment: Altruism as a function of age and aggression. *Journal of Personality and Social Psychology*, 1972, *22*, 139-148.

Grusec, J. W., & Skubiski, S. L. Model nurturance, demand characteristics of the modeling experiment, and altruism. *Journal of Personality and Social Psychology*, 1970, *14*, 352-359.

Handlon, B. J., & Gross, P. The development of sharing behavior. *Journal of Abnormal and Social Psychology*, 1959, *59*, 425-428.

Harré, R., & Secord, P. F. *The explanation of social behavior.* Totowa, N.J.: Rowman & Littlefield, 1972.

Harris, D. B. A scale for measuring attitudes of social responsibility in children. *Journal of Abnormal and Social Psychology*, 1957, *55*, 322-326.

Harris, M. B. Reciprocity and generosity: Some determinants of sharing in children. *Child Development*, 1970, *41* 313-328.

Harris, M. B. The effects of performing one altruistic act on the likelihood of performing another. *Journal of Social Psychology*, 1972, *88*, 65-73.

Hartup, W. W., & Coates, B. Imitation of a peer as a function of reinforcement from the peer group and rewardingness of the model. *Child Development*, 1967, *38*, 1003-1016.

Heider, F. *The psychology of interpersonal relations.* New York: Wiley, 1958.

Hetherington, E. M., & Parke, R. D. *Child psychology: A contemporary viewpoint.* New York: McGraw-Hill, 1975.

Hochreich, D. J. *A children's scale for measuring interpersonal trust.* Unpublished master's thesis, University of Connecticut, 1966.

Hoffman, M. L. Altruistic behavior and the parent-child relationship. *Journal of Personality and Social Psychology*, 1975, *31*, 937-943.

Homans, G. C. Social behavior as exchange. *American Journal of Sociology*, 1958, *62*, 597-606.

Homans, G. C. *Social behavior: Its elementary forms.* New York: Harcourt, Brace & World, 1961.

Hornstein, H. A. The influence of social models on helping. In J. Macaulay & L. Berkowitz (Eds.), *Altruism and helping behavior.* New York: Academic Press, 1970.

Hornstein, H. A., Fisch, E., & Holmes, M. The influence of a model's feeling about his behavior and his relevance as a comparison on other observers' helping behavior. *Journal of Personality and Social Psychology*, 1968, *10*, 222-226.

Horowitz, I. A. Effect of choice and locus of dependence on helping behavior. *Journal of Personality and Social Psychology*, 1968, *8*, 373-376.

Isen, A. M. Success, failure, attention and reaction to others: The warm glow of success. *Journal of Personality and Social Psychology*, 1970, *15*, 294-301.

Isen, A. M., & Levin, P. F. The effect of feeling good on helping: Cookies and kindness. *Journal of Personality and Social Psychology*, 1972, *21*, 384-388.

Jones, E. E., & Davis, K. E. From acts to dispositions. In L. Berkowitz (Ed.), *Advances in experimental social psychology* (Vol. 2). New York: Academic Press, 1965.

Jones, E. E., & Gerard, H. B. *Foundations of social psychology.* New York: Wiley, 1967.

Jones, R. A. Volunteering to help: The effects of choice, dependence and anticipated dependence. *Journal of Personality and Social Psychology*, 1970, *14*, 121-129.

Kahn, A., & Tice, T. E. Returning a favor and retaliating harm: The effects of stated intentions and actual behavior. *Journal of Experimental and Social Psychology*, 1973, *9*, 43-56.

Karabenick, S. A., Lerner, R. M., & Beecher, M. D. Relation of political affiliation to helping behavior on election day, November 7, 1972. *Journal of Social Psychology*, 1973, *91*, 223-227.

Kazdin, A. E., & Bryan, J. H. Competence and volunteering. *Journal of Experimental Social Psychology*, 1971, *7*, 87-97.

Kohlberg, L. Stage and sequence: The cognitive-developmental approach to socialization. In D. Goslin (Ed.), *Handbook of socialization theory and research.* Chicago: Rand McNally, 1969.

Konečni, V. J. Some effects of guilt on compliance: A field replication. *Journal of Personality and Social Psychology*, 1972, *23*, 30-32.

Korte, C. Effects of individual responsibility and group communication on help-giving in an emergency. *Human Relations*, 1971, *24*, 149-159.

Kraut, R. E. Effects of social labeling on giving to charity. *Journal of Experimental Social Psychology*, 1973, *9*, 551-562.

Krebs, D. L. Altruism—An examination of the concept and a review of the literature. *Psychological Bulletin*, 1970, *73*, 258-302.

Krech, D., Crutchfield, R. S., & Ballachey, E. L. *Individual in society: A textbook of social psychology.* New York: McGraw-Hill, 1962.

Kriss, M., Indenbaum, E., & Tesch, F. Message type and status of interactants as determinants of telephone helping behavior. *Journal of Personality and Social Psychology*, 1974, *30*, 856-859.

L'Armand, K., & Pepitone, A. Helping to reward another person: A cross-cultural analysis. *Journal of Personality and Social Psychology*, 1975, *31*, 189-198.

Latané, B. Field studies of altruistic compliance. *Representative Research in Social Psychology*, 1970, *1*, 49–62.

Latané, B., & Darley, J. M. Group inhibition of bystander intervention in emergencies. *Journal of Personality and Social Psychology*, 1968, *10*, 215–221.

Latané, B., & Darley, J. M. Social determinants of bystander intervention in emergencies. In J. Macauley & L. Berkowitz (Eds.), *Altruism and helping behavior.* New York: Academic Press, 1970.

Latané, B., & Rodin, J. A lady in distress: Inhibiting effects of friends and strangers on bystander intervention. *Journal of Experimental Social Psychology*, 1969, *5*, 189–202.

Lazarus, R. S. Emotions and adaptation: Conceptual and empirical relations. In W. J. Arnold (Ed.), *Nebraska Symposium on Motivation* (Vol. 16). Lincoln: University of Nebraska Press, 1968.

Leeds, R. Altruism and the norm of giving. *Merrill-Palmer Quarterly*, 1963, *9*, 229–240.

Lerner, M. J. The desire for justice and reactions to victims. In J. Macaulay & L. Berkowitz (Eds.), *Altruism and helping behavior.* New York: Academic Press, 1970.

Lerner, J. J., & Matthews, G. Reactions to suffering of others under conditions of indirect responsibility. *Journal of Personality and Social Psychology*, 1967, *5*, 319–325.

Leventhal, G. S., Weiss, T., & Long, G. Equity, reciprocity, and reallocating rewards in the dyad. *Journal of Personality and Social Psychology*, 1969, *13*, 300–305.

Levy, P., Lundgren, D., Ansel, M., Fell, D., Fink, B., & McGrath, J. E. Bystander effect in a demand-without-threat situation. *Journal of Personality and Social Psychology*, 1972, *24*, 166–171.

Liebhart, E. H. Empathy and emergency helping: The effects of personality, self-concern, and acquaintance. *Journal of Experimental Social Psychology*, 1972, *8*, 404–411.

London, P. The rescuers: Motivational hypotheses about Christians who saved Jews from the Nazis. In J. Macaulay & L. Berkowitz (Eds.), *Altruism and helping behavior.* New York: Academic Press, 1970.

Lowe, R., & Ritchey, G. Relation of altruism to age, social class, and ethnic identity. *Psychological Reports*, 1973, *33*, 567–572.

Macaulay, J. R. A shill for charity. In J. Macaulay & L. Berkowitz (Eds.), *Altruism and helping behavior.* New York: Academic Press, 1970.

Macaulay, J. R., & Berkowitz, L. (Eds.), *Altruism and helping behavior.* New York: Academic Press, 1970.

McCandless, B. R., & Evans, E. D. *Children and youth: Psychosocial development.* Hinsdale, Ill.: Dryden Press, 1973.

McGuire, W. J. The yin and yang of progress in social psychology: Seven koan. *Journal of Personality and Social Psychology*, 1973, *26*, 446–456.

McMillen, D. L. Transgression, self-image, and compliant behavior. *Journal of Personality and Social Psychology*, 1971, *20*, 176–179.

McMillen, D. L., & Austin, J. B. Effect of positive feedback on compliance following transgression. *Psychonomic Science*, 1971, *24*, 59–61.

Middlebrook, P. N. *Social psychology and modern life.* New York: Alfred A. Knopf, 1974.

Midlarsky, E. Aiding responses: An analysis and review. *Merill-Palmer Quarterly*, 1968, *14*, 229–260.

Midlarsky, E., & Bryan, J. H. Training charity in children. *Journal of Personality and Social Psychology*, 1967, *5*, 408–415.

Midlarsky, E., & Bryan, J. H. Affect expressions and children's imitative altruism. *Journal of Experimental Research in Personality*, 1972, *6*, 195–203.

Midlarsky, E., Bryan, J. H., & Brickman, P. Aversive approval: Interactive effects of modeling and reinforcement on altruistic behavior. *Child Development*, 1973, *44*, 321–328.

Milgram, S. The experience of living in cities. *Science*, 1970, *167*, 1461–1468.

Miller, N. E., & Dollard, J. *Social learning and imitation.* New Haven: Yale University Press, 1941.

Mischel, W. *Personality and assessment.* New York: Wiley, 1968.

Mischel, W. Continuity and change in personality. *American Psychologist*, 1969, *24*, 1012–1018.

Mischel, W. *Introduction to personality.* New York: Holt, Rinehart & Winston, 1971.

Mischel, W. Toward a cognitive social learning reconceptualization of personality. *Psychological Review*, 1973, *80*, 252-283.

Morgan, W. G. Situational specificity in altruistic behavior. *Journal of Representative Research in Social Psychology*, 1973, *4*, 56-66.

Moss, M. K., & Page, R. A. Reinforcement and helping behavior. *Journal of Applied Social Psychology*, 1972, 2, 360-371.

Mowrer, O. H. *Learning theory and personality dynamics.* New York: Ronald Press, 1950.

Muir, D. E., & Weinstein, E. A. The social debt: An investigation of lower-class and middle-class norms of social obligation. *American Sociological Review*, 1962, 27, 532-539.

Mussen, P. H., Conger, J. J., & Kagan, J. *Child development and personality* (4th ed.). New York: Harper & Row, 1974.

Mussen, P., Harris, S., Rutherford, E., & Keasey, C. B. Honesty and altruism among preadolesants. *Developmental Psychology*, 1970, *3*, 169-194.

Nacci, P., Stapleton, R. E., & Tedeschi, J. T. An empirical restatement of the reciprocity norms. *Journal of Social Psychology*, 1973, *91*, 263-271.

Nadler, A., Fisher, J. D., & Streufert, S. The donor's dilemma: Recipient's reactions to aid from friend or foe. *Journal of Applied Social Psychology*, 1974, *4*, 275-285.

Nemeth, C. Bargaining and reciprocity. *Psychological Bulletin*, 1970, *74*, 297-308. (a)

Nemeth, C. Effects of free versus constrained behavior on attraction between people. *Journal of Personality and Social Psychology*, 1970, *15*, 302-311. (b)

Orne, M. T., & Evans, F. J. Social control in the psychological experiment: Antisocial behavior and hypnosis. *Journal of Personality and Social Psychology*, 1965, *1*, 189-200.

Penner, L. A., Dertke, M. C., & Achenbach, C. J. The "flash" system: A field study of altruism. *Journal of Applied Social Psychology*, 1973, *3*, 362-370.

Piaget, J. *The moral judgment of the child.* London: K. Paul, Trench, Trubner, & Co., 1932.

Piliavin, J. A., & Piliavin, I. M. The effect of blood on reactions to a victim. *Journal of Personality and Social Psychology*, 1972, *23*, 353-361.

Piliavin, I. M., Rodin, J., & Piliavin, J. A. Good samaritanism: An underground phenomenon? *Journal of Personality and Social Psychology*, 1969, *13*, 289–299.

Pliner, P., Hart, H., Kohl, J., & Saari, D. Compliance without pressure: Some further data on the foot-in-the-door technique. *Journal of Experimental Social Psychology*, 1974, *10*, 17–22.

Pomazal, R. J., & Clore, G. L. Helping on the highway: The effects of dependency and sex. *Journal of Applied Social Psychology*, 1973, *3*, 150–164.

Pruitt, D. G. Reciprocity and credit building in a laboratory dyad. *Journal of Personality and Social Psychology*, 1968, *8*, 143–147.

Rawlings, E. I. Witnessing harm to other: A reassessment of the role of guilt in altruistic behavior. *Journal of Personality and Social Psychology*, 1968, *10*, 377–380.

Rawlings, E. I. Reactive guilt and anticipatory guilt in altruistic behavior. In J. Macaulay & L. Berkowitz (Eds.), *Altruism and helping behavior*. New York: Academic Press, 1970.

Regan, D. T. Effects of a favor and liking on compliance. *Journal of Experimental Social Psychology*, 1971, *7*, 627–639.

Regan, D. T., Williams, M., & Sparling, S. Voluntary expiation of guilt: A field experiment. *Journal of Personality and Social Psychology*, 1972, *24*, 42–45.

Rosenhan, D. Some origins of concern for others. In P. H. Mussen, J. Langer, & M. Covington (Eds.), *Trends and issues in developmental psychology*. New York: Holt, Rinehart & Winston, 1969.

Rosenhan, D. The natural socialization of altruistic autonomy. In J. Macaulay & L. Berkowitz (Eds.), *Altruism and helping behavior*. New York: Academic Press, 1970.

Rosenhan, D. L. Learning theory and prosocial behavior. *Journal of Social Issues*, 1972, *28*(3), 151–163.

Rosenhan, D. L., Underwood, B., & Moore, B. Affect moderates self-gratification and altruism. *Journal of Personality and Social Psychology*, 1974, *30*, 546–552.

Rosenhan, D., & White, G. M. Observation and rehearsal as determinants of prosocial behavior. *Journal of Personality and Social Psychology*, 1967, *5*, 424–431.

Rosenthal, A. M. *Thirty-eight witnesses.* New York: McGraw-Hill, 1964.

Ross, A. S. Effect of increased responsibility on bystander intervention: The presence of children. *Journal of Personality and Social Psychology,* 1971, *19,* 306-310.

Ross, A. S., & Braband, Y. Effect of increased responsibility on bystander intervention, II: The cue value of a blind person. *Journal of Personality and Social Psychology,* 1973, *25,* 254-258.

Rubin, K. H., & Schneider, F. W. The relationship between moral judgment, egocentrism, and altruistic behavior. *Child Development,* 1973, *44,* 661-665.

Rushton, J. P. Generosity in children: Immediate and long-term effects of modeling, preaching, and moral judgment. *Journal of Personality and Social Psychology,* 1975, *31,* 459-466.

Rutherford, E., & Mussen, P. Generosity in nursery school boys. *Child Development,* 1968, *39,* 755-765.

Sawyer, J. The altruism scale: A measure of cooperative, individualistic, and competitive interpersonal orientation. *American Journal of Sociology,* 1966, *71,* 407-416.

Saxe, L., & Greenberg, M. *Reaction to a help attempt: Importance of locus of help initiation and nature of outcome.* Paper presented at the meeting of the Eastern Psychological Association, Philadelphia, 1974.

Schachter, S. The interaction of cognitive and physiological determinants of emotional state. In L. Berkowitz (Ed.), *Advances in experimental social psychology* (Vol. 1). New York: Academic Press, 1964.

Schaeffer, D. *Effects of reciprocity and third-party compensation on helping behavior.* Unpublished master's thesis, University of Pittsburgh, 1975.

Schaps, E. Cost, dependency, and helping. *Journal of Personality and Social Psychology,* 1972, *21,* 74-78.

Schopler, J. An investigation of sex differences on the influence of dependence. *Sociometry,* 1967, *30,* 50-63.

Schopler, J. An attribution analysis of some determinants of reciprocating a benefit. In J. Macaulay & L. Berkowitz (Eds.), *Altruism and helping behavior.* New York: Academic Press, 1970.

Schopler, J., & Bateson, N. The power of dependence.

Journal of Personality and Social Psychology, 1965, *2*, 247-254.

Schopler, J., & Matthews, M. W. The influence of the perceived causal locus of partner's dependence on the use of interpersonal power. *Journal of Personality and Social Psychology*, 1965, *2*, 609-612.

Schopler, J., & Thompson, V. D. The role of attribution processes in mediating amount of reciprocity for a favor. *Journal of Personality and Social Psychology*, 1968, *10*, 243-250.

Schwartz, S. H. Awareness of consequences and the influence of moral norms on interpersonal behavior. *Sociometry*, 1968, *31*, 355-369.

Schwartz, S. H. Moral decision making and behavior. In J. Macaulay & L. Berkowitz (Eds.), *Altruism and helping behavior*. New York: Academic Press, 1970.

Schwartz, S. H. Normative explanations of helping behavior: A critique, proposal, and empirical test. *Journal of Experimental Social Psychology*, 1973, *9*, 349-364.

Schwartz, S. H., & Clausen, G. T. Responsibility, norms, and helping in an emergency. *Journal of Personality and Social Psychology*, 1970, *16*, 299-310.

Sharabany, R. *The development of intimacy among children in the kibbutz.* Paper presented at the biennial meeting of the International Society for the Study of Behavioral Development, Ann Arbor, Mich., August 1973.

Sharabany, R. *Intimate friendship among kibbutz and city children and its measurement.* Unpublished doctoral dissertation, Cornell University, 1974. (University Microfilms No. 74-17, 682)

Sherrod, D. R., & Downs, R. Environmental determinants of altruism: The effects of stimulus overload and perceived control on helping. *Journal of Experimental Social Psychology*, 1974, *10*, 468-479.

Silverman, I. W. Incidence of guilt reactions in children. *Journal of Personality and Social Psychology*, 1967, *7*, 338-340.

Smith, R. E., Smythe, L., & Lien, D. Inhibition of helping behavior by a similar or dissimiliar nonreactive fellow bystander. *Journal of Personality and Social Psychology*, 1972, *23*, 414-420.

Smith, R. E., Vanderbilt, K., & Callen, M. B. Social comparison and bystander intervention in emergencies. *Journal of Applied Social Psychology*, 1973, *3*, 186-196.

Snyder, M., & Cunningham, M. R. To comply or not comply: Testing the self-perception explanation of the "foot-in-the-door" phenomenon. *Journal of Personality and Social Psychology*, 1975, *31*, 64-67.

Sole, K., Marton, J., & Hornstein, H. A. Opinion similarity and helping: Three field experiments investigating the bases of promotive tension. *Journal of Experimental Social Psychology*, 1975, *11*, 1-13.

Stapleton, R. E., Nacci, P., & Tedeschi, J. T. Interpersonal attraction and the reciprocation of benefits. *Journal of Personality and Social Psychology*, 1973, *28*, 199-205.

Staub, E. A child in distress: The effect of focusing responsibility on children on their attempts to help. *Developmental Psychology*, 1970, *2*, 152-153. (a)

Staub, E. A child in distress: The influence of age and number of witnesses on children's attempts to help. *Journal of Personality and Social Psychology*, 1970, *14*, 130-140.(b)

Staub, E. A child in distress: The influence of nurturance and modeling on children's attempts to help. *Developmental Psychology*, 1971, *5*, 124-132. (a)

Staub, E. Helping a person in distress: The influence of implicit and explicit "rules" of conduct on children and adults. *Journal of Personality and Social Psychology*, 1971, *17*, 137-144. (b)

Staub, E. The use of role playing and induction in children's learning of helping and sharing behavior. *Child Development*, 1971, *42*, 805-816.(c)

Staub, E. Instigation to goodness: The role of social norms and interpersonal influence. *Journal of Social Issues*, 1972, *28*(3), 131-150.

Staub, E. Helping a distressed person: Social, personality, and stimulus determinants. In L. Berkowitz (Ed.), *Advances in experimental social psychology* (Vol. 7). New York: Academic Press, 1974.

Staub, E., & Baer, R. S., Jr. Stimulus characteristics of a sufferer and difficulty of escape as determinants of helping. *Journal of Personality and Social Psychology*, 1974, *30*, 279-284.

Staub, E., & Sherk, L. Need for approval, children's sharing behavior, and reciprocity in sharing. *Child Development*, 1970, *41*, 243–252.

Stevenson, H. W. Social reinforcement of children's behavior. In L. P. Lipsitt & C. C. Spiler (Eds.), *Advances in child development and behavior* (Vol. 2). New York: Academic Press, 1965.

Suedfeld, P., Bochner, S., & Wnek, D. Helper-sufferer similarity and a specific request for help: Bystander intervention during a peace demonstration. *Journal of Applied Social Psychology*, 1972, *2*, 17–23.

Tesser, A., Gatewood, R., & Driver, M. Some determinants of gratitude. *Journal of Personality and Social Psychology*, 1968, *9*, 233–236.

Thayer, S. Lend me your ears: Racial and sexual factors in helping the deaf. *Journal of Personality and Social Psychology*, 1973, *28*, 8–11.

Thibaut, J. W., & Kelley, H. H. *The social psychology of groups.* New York: Wiley, 1959.

Thibaut, J. W., & Riecken, H. W. Some determinants and consequences of the perception of social causality. *Journal of Personality*, 1955, *24*, 113–133.

Thompson, V. D., Stroebe, W., & Schopler, J. Some situational determinants of the motives attributed to the person who performs a helping act. *Journal of Personality*, 1971, *39*, 460–472.

Tipton, R. M., & Browning, S. The influence of age and obesity on helping behavior. *British Journal of Social and Clinical Psychology*, 1972, *11*, 404–406.

Ugurel-Semin, R. Moral behavior and moral judgment of children. *Journal of Abnormal and Social Psychology*, 1952, *47*, 463–474.

Uranowitz, S. W. Helping and self-attributions: A field experiment. *Journal of Personality and Social Psychology*, 1975, *31*, 852–854.

Wagner, C., & Wheeler, L. Model, need, and cost effects in helping behavior. *Journal of Personality and Social Psychology*, 1969, *12* 111–116.

Wallace, J., & Sadalla, E. Behavioral consequences of transgression: I. The effects of social recognition. *Journal of Experimental Research in Personality*, 1966, *1*, 187-194.

Walster, E., Berscheid, E., & Walster, G. W. The exploited: Justice or justification? In J. Macaulay & L. Berkowitz (Eds.), *Altruism and helping behavior*. New York: Academic Press, 1970.

Walster, E., Berscheid, E., & Walster, G. W. New directions in equity research. *Journal of Personality and Social Psychology*, 1973, *25*, 151-176.

Walster, E., & Piliavin, J. A. Equity and the innocent bystander. *Journal of Social Issues*, 1972, *28*(3), 165-189.

Walster, E., & Prestholdt, P. The effect of misjudging another: Overcompensation or dissonance reduction? *Journal of Experimental Social Psychology*, 1966, *2*, 85-97.

Walster, E., Walster, B., Abrahams, D., & Brown, Z. The effect on liking of underrating or overrating another. *Journal of Experimental Social Psychology*, 1966, *2*, 70-84.

West, S. G., Whitney, G., & Schnedler, R. Helping a motorist in distress: The effects of sex, race, and neighborhood. *Journal of Personality and Social Psychology*, 1975, *31*, 691-698.

Wilke, H., & Lanzetta, J. T. The obligation to help: The effects of amount of prior help on subsequent helping behavior. *Journal of Experimental Social Psychology*, 1970, *6*, 488-493.

Willis, J. A., & Goethals, G. R. Social responsibility and threat to behavioral freedom as determinants of altruistic behavior. *Journal of Personality*, 1973, *41*, 376-384.

Wispé, L. G. Positive forms of social behavior: An overview. *Journal of Social Issues*, 1972, *28*(3), 1-19.

Wispé, L. G., & Freshley, H. B. Race, sex, and sympathetic helping behavior: The broken bag caper. *Journal of Personality and Social Psychology*, 1971, *17*, 59-65.

Wright, B. Altruism in children and perceived conduct of others. *Journal of Abnormal and Social Psychology*, 1942, *37*, 218-233.

Yakimovich, D., & Saltz, E. Helping behavior: The cry for help. *Psychonomic Science*, 1971, *23*, 427-428.

Yarrow, M. R., Scott, P. M., & Waxler, C. Z. Learning concern for others. *Developmental Psychology*, 1973, *8*, 240-260.

AUTHOR INDEX

Numbers in italics refer to the pages on which the complete references are cited.

SUBJECT INDEX

Adequacy of compensation,
142–143
Age
and nonemergency altruistic
behavior, 62, 77
and prosocial behavior, 11–14
Aggression vs. prosocial behavior,
4
Altruism
and age, 12, 14
and empathy, 49
and modeling consistency,
26–27
as prosocial behavior, 5–7
and reciprocity, 40
(*See also* Altruistic behavior;
Prosocial behavior)
Altruism Scale, 64
Altruistic behavior
and awareness of need, 52,
54–56
and cognitive development,
16–17
and cost-reward analysis, 52,
58–60
cultural approach, 47–49
decision-making process of,
52–54
developmental approach, 46–47
exchange approach, 39–42
judgmental process, 52, 56–60

and locus of dependency, 57–58
and moralism, 34–35
normative approach, 42–46
observation, and nonemergency
judgments, 66–68
personal variables, 52, 60–65
teaching methods, 31–33
and vicarious reinforcement, 23
(*See also* Altruism; Prosocial
behavior)
Altruistic norm, and reciprocity
behavior, 118
Antecedents
familial, and prosocial behavior,
33–36
investigation, in prosocial behavior studies, 150–151
Ascription of Responsibility Scale,
103
Autonomous morality, 15–16
Awareness
and giving interaction, in prosocial behavior, 154–155
and helping in emergency,
88–89, 98–99
of need, and altruistic behavior,
52, 54–56

Behavior
causal locus, 57

191